PONDER
AND PRAY

PONDER AND PRAY

SEVEN WEEKS

OF

MEDITATIONS

AND PRAYERS

FOR

PERSONAL

ENRICHMENT

VICTOR SHEPHERD

CLEMENTS
PUBLISHING
Toronto

Ponder and Pray

Copyright © 2002 by Victor A. Shepherd

This edition published 2002 by
Clements Publishing
Box 213, 6021 Yonge Street
Toronto, Ontario M2M 3W2 Canada
www.clementspublishing.com

Cover design by Davis

Canadian Cataloguing in Publication Data

Shepherd, Victor A., 1944–
Ponder and pray:
seven weeks of meditations and prayers for personal enrichment

ISBN 1-894667-03-4

1. Meditations. 2. Prayers. I. Title.

BV4811.S44 2002   242'.2   C00-932803-3

In gratitude for

EMIL L. FACKENHEIM

philosopher, professor, rabbi, friend,

– and survivor of Sachsenhausen –

from whom I learned,

"Prayer is the quintessential human act."

CONTENTS

CONTENTS

Preface

If the number of books on prayer is any indication, ministers relentlessly urge their people to pray. The same ministers, I have found, seem not to understand that most people find prayer difficult, "run out of words" quickly, feel guilty because they don't know what to say next, and soon weary of dredging up words that seem as far off as the spring is in the middle of winter. Their people quit praying.

In preparing a devotional book that Christians of almost any age, stage, education or persuasion could use, I have kept in mind the need to provide assistance for people who find the task of "composing" prayers challenging. For this reason I have been as painstaking with the prayers as I have been with the expositions that form the background to the reader's intercessions. It is hoped that the printed prayers will provide enough encouragement to keep people praying who would otherwise give up.

The expositions explore well-known incidents in the earthly ministry of Jesus (e.g., his encounter with Nicodemus), as well as the principal words associated with the Christian faith (e.g., "love"), even as the biblical meaning of those words often varies widely from popular understanding.

The book is dedicated to Emil Fackenheim. He was an internationally acclaimed professor of philosophy at the University of Toronto when I studied philosophy there as both an undergraduate and a graduate student. In him I found intellectual brilliance combined with the profoundest confidence in the Holy One of Israel. It all left me fervent in faith and ardent in philosophy. My debt to him is unpayable.

—Victor Shepherd

DAY 1

THE AUTHORITY OF JESUS CHRIST (1)

Luke 5:17-24

Authoritarian people are tyrants. They threaten. Often they brutalize. They are feared but never respected, loved or trusted. Jesus Christ is not authoritarian. But he is authoritative; that is, he has a unique effectiveness which we recognize. We trust him. He can only enhance our good.

During our Lord's earthly ministry it was recognized that "he has authority on earth to forgive sins." His distinctive effectiveness here is vital, for so much human distress is linked to people's reluctance to be forgiven. So much anxiety is really a disguised form of guilt, as well as much nagging depression. And how much compulsive perfectionism, with its strength-sapping fussiness and its constant headaches, is rooted in our not being able to forgive ourselves, which is to say, in our not having found ourselves forgiven?

My wife and I were startled one evening at the behaviour of our eight year old daughter. She volunteered to wash and dry the supper dishes, and did so. Then she washed the top of the refrigerator with the dishcloth. Next she tidied the living room, putting all the old newspapers in one corner. Finally she told us she had misbehaved badly at school that day, and during lunch hour had been made to stand in the hall. We smile as we see the compulsive achievement, the perfectionism, which is offered to her parents (and to herself) as compensation for her guilt. But adults do as much even if the mechanism with us is largely unconscious. We do as much to promote acceptance with God or with life in general and with ourselves. Adults tend to oscillate between compulsive perfectionism and nagging depression or self-contempt

(where the perfectionist mechanism isn't used.)

Yet Jesus Christ has authority to forgive. Finding ourselves forgiven we know ourselves accepted by him and therefore acceptable to ourselves. Now we see that our compulsive perfectionism is unnecessary, our depression groundless, and our fussy anxiety superfluous. Genuine authority is always genuinely helpful.

Prayer

Eternal God, you are greater than we can imagine and mightier than we can conceive, yet you have come to us in Christ Jesus to share our life and our lot. We praise you that in him we have found you our rightful ruler whose lordship we clearly recognize,

gladly assent to,
and humbly honour.

Magnify our confidence in the pardon our Saviour presses upon us.
> *When we think we are unforgivable, dispel our inverted*
> > *pride.*
>
> *When we feel we need no forgiveness, acquaint us with*
> > *our secret faults.*
>
> *When we hesitate to forgive others, remind us that*
> > *forgivingness and forgivenness are together the seamless*
> > *robe which your people are given to put on.*

Take from us the compulsiveness which denies your free
> > *acceptance of us;*
> > > *the guilt which we cling to because it seems to*
> > > *compensate for our sin;*
> > > *the silliness that our faultlessness will one day*
> > > *guarantee our standing with you;*
> > > *the fussiness which points to an inner disquiet*
> > > > *where there should be the joy of the*
> > > > *person set free.*

---

*As we hear our Lord pronounce us his people, as we see him
enfold us in his mercy,*
> *grant us assurance that he has received us and will never
>> let us go;*
> *grant us confidence that we can always take him at his
>> word;*
> *grant us boldness to affirm ourselves as those creatures
>> with whom he is forever pleased,
>> to whom he has promised his peace,
>> into whom he now pours his power.*

*We pray in the certainty that you, our God, are the one whose
face is mirrored in the face of Jesus Christ, and whose face will
ever shine upon us. Amen.*

DAY 2

THE AUTHORITY OF JESUS CHRIST (2)

Mark 1:22

People recognized a unique effectiveness in Christ's teaching, "...for he taught them as one who had authority, and not as the scribes." The scribes were often authoritarian. They laid unbearable burdens on people and then did nothing to ease them. They were hair-splitters. Failure to embark on their "trip" marked one out as personally defective and spiritually deficient. People resented the authoritarianism of the scribes, yet they were astonished at the authority of Jesus' teaching. His had the ring of truth about it.

If you place two violins side by side and then draw the bow across one string of one violin only, that one string will vibrate and produce a note. Immediately the same string on the second violin will begin to vibrate and produce the same note even though the bow hasn't touched it. The sound in the second violin is produced by a sympathetic vibration. A sympathetic vibration is called resonance. When Jesus taught, people felt in themselves a sympathetic vibration. They resonated with his teaching. "That's it!", they cried, "We recognize its truth."

Today authoritarian institutions and individuals shout advice as to how we are to run our lives. Just as we begin to feel overwhelmed by their clamour and shrillness, we hear our Lord himself. And once more we resonate with his teaching. It has a unique effectiveness with us. We recognize the ring of truth in what he says about acquisitiveness, grudge-holding, faithlessness and the unforgiving spirit, even as we recognize the realism in his word about mercy, forthrightness, generosity and single-mindedness.

Jesus Christ speaks quietly just because he doesn't need to shout. The weight of his teaching is conveyed entirely by its authority. We resonate with the teaching as we trust the teacher himself.

Prayer

Gracious God, you have never left your people to grope and stumble but have always declared to us your will for us and your way with us. We praise you that in the teaching of our Lord Jesus Christ you have made plain the road we are to walk and the road we are to shun. Today we ask you to illuminate afresh for us the word we must hide in our hearts that it might direct us until our life's end. Sensitize our hearing, we ask, that nothing we need to hear we shall fail to hear.

Where we are deafened through our own wilfulness, give
us to see that we are never so free as when we will
to honour our Lord and his way.
Where we are deafened by the world's clamour and clatter,
direct us to that still small voice whose whisper is
more telling than the surrounding din.
Where we are deafened by that temptation whose first
work is to blunt our hearing of our Lord, unstop
our ears before we stumble and fall.

Save us, we ask, from hearing only the teaching which comforts while ignoring the word which confronts:
that the earth is yours and is not ours to pollute;
that our assailants must hear our word of pardon;
that tattered clothing merely covers those whom your kingdom
calls "royal;"
that our assistance to the homeless and
our kindness to the imprisoned and
our selflessness before the wretched of the
world are the measure of our love for our Lord.

Gracious God, the Hebrew language of your word written

*reminds us that obedience is but intensified hearing, and hearing
is the first step of obedience. Then invigorate our obedience, we
plead, for it is in obeying you that our faith is strengthened;*

> *it is in obeying you that we learn why your truth is our
> guide;*
> *it is in obeying you that each step we take is granted
> light enough for the next step as well.*

*As we listen to our Lord Jesus, let our hearts and minds resonate
with his, for then we shall see the truth,*

> *know the truth, and*
> *do the truth,*
> *only to find increasing day by day our love for him who
> is the truth. Amen.*

DAY 3

THE AUTHORITY OF JESUS CHRIST (3)

Luke 4:31-36

People recognized a unique effectiveness in Christ's power. "And they were all amazed…for with authority and power he commands the unclean spirits, and they come out." We too have unclean spirits, and we do indeed need deliverance. "For out of the heart of men and women come fornication, theft, murder, coveting, deceit, slander, adultery, arrogance." Nothing less than deliverance will do.

Yet deliverance isn't always what we long for. A startling instance of this is the teenager who suffers from anorexia nervosa, the psychiatric ailment which finds her thinking she is overweight when in fact she is as skinny as a rake. She refuses to eat, getting sicker and scrawnier by the day. It would always be possible to sedate the sufferer and force feed her, but such a move would be very authoritarian, and besides, it would solve nothing in the long run. Recently I heard of one such person whom no one could get to eat. Last summer, even though her health was precarious, she went away to a summer camp. There she found herself among happy, healthy young women who exemplified for her what she longed for, unconsciously, but had never been able to admit. Something "clicked" inside her. She began to eat.

Something like this happens to us adults. In our spiritual perversity what we need most in life we most perversely reject. Yet as we live in the company of Jesus Christ and his people we shall catch sight of his humanness, ordinary as ours is ordinary yet winsomely authentic. Seeing in his humanness the fulfillment of our own, we shall want to be rid of our unclean spirits. We shall cling to him, and cling even more tightly to him, and find in our intimacy with him the deliverance we need.

Of course we should esteem the learning of the learned and the achievement of the achievers. But what should move us most are the people, learned or not, who have found in the gospel of Jesus Christ deliverance of any sort, however undramatic. For they have firsthand acquaintance with the one whose authority never tyrannizes but instead frees us as it releases us from all that enslaves.

Prayer

Eternal God, you have not held yourself from us but have come down among us in love and truth and power. We praise you for the earthly ministry of our Lord wherein the infirm found healing of body, mind and spirit.
> *Increase our confidence in your purpose for us and your*
>> *power within us.*
> *Enlarge our trust in you in all times and places;*
> *Swell our gratitude as we glory in your deliverance*
>> *of us from our manifold twistedness.*

We confess that the greatest impediment to our restoration is our unwillingness to let go of the very thing from which we need to be freed, for
> *hatred can motivate us as little else often does;*
> *revenge can delight us more than we care to admit;*
> *lust can fascinate and entertain us endlessly, and*
> *negative thinking can become a deadly rut.*

We intercede for those areas of the world where evil surges and where your people need to be lifted up:
>> *—Northern Ireland, with its centuries-old stand-off of*
>>> *shocking animosity,*
>> *— Russia and its neighbours whose economic woes render*
>>> *communism's return attractive,*
>> *—the Near East, with its tensions and turmoils,*

*—our own land, where infestation of evil is easier to
overlook, and where injustice is more readily
rationalized.*

*Just as you have commissioned your people to cast out the spirits
in your name, so equip us to be agents of your justice and your
peace.*

*We thank you for the great cloud of witnesses by whom we are
surrounded and whose persistent presence encourages us and
cheers us:*
    *the man whose deliverance from addiction lends hope to the
        enslaved;*
    *the woman whose deliverance from nastiness will encourage the
        embittered;*
    *the person who can gently say to all detractors, "I was blind, I
        can see, and I know it"—and who will impel us to keep
        clinging to our Lord and keep pointing others to him.*

*We offer our prayer knowing that you long for our deliverance
with a passion which is even now quickening ours. Amen.*

DAY 4

NICODEMUS (1)
John 3:1-21

"Born again." One word in Greek, two small words in English, the expression used in this form is found only once in Scripture. In one corner is the champion of the "twice-born," declaring that unless we use the words we aren't genuinely spiritual. In the other corner is the challenger, insisting that if we do use the words we aren't intellectually profound. We are saddened at the stand-off, for the cause of Christ is never advanced when two opponents square off. The cause of Christ is advanced only as champion and challenger drop their hostility and reflect together on what birth means in everyday life.

Birth is obviously a change of context. When a baby is born the context changes from amniotic fluid to air, from confinement to freedom, from silence to exclamation, from darkness to light. Our changed context is the sphere, the atmosphere, of the Triune God as the Father's splendour bleaches our shadow-side, the Son's humility undoes our self-seeking, and the Spirit's wooing finds us welcoming what we now see not to violate us. The birth of which Jesus speaks finds the spiritual newborn opening up to God as surely as a cellar-bound plant turns to the sun when brought into the light. Surely there is nothing bizarre or puzzling about this. There may be an unusual inner experience accompanying such a change, but certainly there needn't be and we shouldn't go looking for it.

When the baby's immediate context changes from amniotic fluid to air, from silence to exclamation, everyone recognizes the change as something which ought to be. No one finds it unusual or unexpected. The child, rather, has moved into that context which is entirely appropriate and certainly necessary for growth and maturity.

To be born of the Spirit is to have one's life unfold in the context of the living God. And this development has always been recognized by God's people as appropriate, expected and necessary.

Prayer

Gracious God, you have told us that you are the one who makes all things new. We praise you that you created us in love and now renew us in mercy. Today we ask you to recall us to that act of power and wonder wherein you granted Jesus, your Son, life anew from the dead, and also to that act of power and wonder wherein you granted us, your children, life anew in him.

Teach us afresh that cold suspicion towards others who call upon his name does not advance his cause.
    When we think others spiritually shallow, remind us that we are not the searchers of people's hearts.
    When we think others intellectually snobbish, remind us that there can be no faith without understanding.
    When we are weary of religious dispute and ready to dismiss the issue of new birth, remind us of your assessment of our predicament, your patience with us and your purpose for us.

Keep before us the vision of that new creation which you have fashioned in the one in whom all things are made new:
    a world where the wolf lies down with the lamb,
    a world where sickness and poverty, hunger and strife are dispelled,
    a world where war isn't learned any more.

And move us to do the truth you have caused us to see that we might hasten the advent of that new heaven and new earth in which righteousness dwells. We ask you to warm us and stir us and enthuse us anew, for then

> *we shall discern your work of grace within us;*
> *we shall encourage each other in the way of a disciple;*
> *we shall plead with those whose ears remain stopped and*
> *whose eyes are closed;*
> *we shall embrace the sons and daughters of the Father's*
> *household, and*
> *we shall rejoice that their names and ours are written in the*
> *Book of Life.*

As we pray, we know that you are ever doing a new thing in our world. We trust you to illumine it for us, and we thank you that you will bring to completion that good work which you have begun in us, in others, and throughout your creation. Amen.

DAY 5

Nicodemus (2)

John 3:1-21

"Nature versus Nurture." This expression is simply another form of the conflict mentioned yesterday. Some argue that we become Christians through an identifiable change in nature. Others argue that it occurs through a steady process of nurture. A moment's reflection lays bare the strength and weakness of each position. Naturists remind nurturists that what passes for Christian nurture is often so dilute, so anemic, that it wouldn't nurture a chickadee; besides, they add, nurture is quite ineffective when it's applied to stillbirths. On the other hand, nurturists remind naturists that some of those who wield the fighting words "born again" like a hammer appear nasty and rude, while others exploit the expression as a political gimmick, bandying it about in sheer self-interest, debasing the words and rendering hearers cynical.

Yet surely there are as many ways of encountering Jesus Christ as there are ways of falling in love. Some people are swept off their feet: love at first sight. Some find their love relationship beginning slowly and developing steadily. Others find that they come to know someone else intimately with much turbulence, with dark moments and doubt, confusion and misunderstanding. But at the end of this up-and-down business there is light and love and life. And two people then step out together into this light and love and life. No one would think of saying, "You can genuinely be in love only if you came to be in love by the route I prescribe."

Exactly how we come to be in Christ doesn't diminish our standing in Christ. The witness of naturist and nurturist alike is to be received and cherished. What matters is that we abide henceforth in our Lord.

Prayer

*Eternal God, you have told us that the kernel of grain which
disappears into the ground you will cause to germinate and bear
fruit. We praise you that you keep the promises you make. We
trust you to fulfill your purpose in us, that we might become men
and women whose usefulness and attractiveness will move others
to know you, trust you, obey you and love you.*

*Today we ask you to increase our confidence in your word and
deed. So cause your word of truth to unfold within us that we
shall be your instrument*
    of clarity to those who are confused,
    of certitude to those who doubt,
    of contentment to those who are agitated,
    of hope to those who see no future.

*Our Lord has taught us that we must continue to abide in him, as
he ever abides in us. Then confirm our dwelling in him*
    as you stabilize us amidst the turbulence we cannot escape,
    as you nourish us with the bread of life,
    as you challenge us with a task worthy of us,
    as you satisfy us with riches available nowhere else.

*We thank you for people whose relationship to us has reflected
your relationship with us:*
    the teacher who corrected us without humiliating us,
    the friend who supported us in dark and dreary days,
    the child who re-acquainted us with life's freshness,
    *the spouse whose faithfulness has strengthened us, startled us
        and comforted us.*

We praise you
    for the light which illumines our path and its pitfalls,
    for the love which greeted us at our birth and will see us

through our dying,
for the life you have lived in our flesh, and which we yearn to
live for ourselves as we, like our Lord, turn hand and
heart to the neighbour whom you have given us today.

We conclude our prayers knowing that you are the one who is,
who was, and who ever shall be. Amen.

DAY 6

Nicodemus (3)

John 3:1-21

"You can't be serious!" gasps Nicodemus. "What do you mean, 'born again'?" Jesus couldn't be more serious. He's talking about something of monumental importance. "Again" or "anew" translates a Greek word with three meanings. It can mean "again" in the sense of "one more time." It can mean "from the beginning, from square one." It can mean "from above, from God." Nicodemus picks out the first meaning only and says to Jesus, with the crudest literalism, "How can I get into my mother's uterus one more time?" He can't, obviously. But Jesus has in mind only the latter two meanings. To be born again is to have life wholly reconstituted, and this from God. Life can be refashioned under God. And people like Nicodemus long for this even if they can't identify their longing and can't articulate it.

More than long for it, we have always pursued it. Different religious customs have been thought to confer it. At the same time as Jesus was conversing earnestly with Nicodemus, devotees of Greek mystery religious cherished an unusual rite. The devotees stood in a pit covered with latticework. A bull was led onto the latticework. Its throat was slashed. As blood poured out over the devotees, they were pronounced "reborn for eternity." While the rite may have been crude, the longing which lay behind it was not. People have always felt after, longed for, the profoundest renewal of themselves and their world.

Right in the midst of our Lord's conversation with Nicodemus the gospel-writer appears to interject inappropriately the lifting up of Jesus, the blood-shedding of the crucified one. But the inappropriateness disappears as we understand that the new context which spells new life is the unrelenting embrace of the one who has given up himself for us and now continues to give himself to us.

What gave the earliest Christians their resilience and credibility was this: they had come to know the one who can grant what all humankind craves.

Prayer

Sovereign eternal, we bow before you.
Lord eternal, we serve you.
Judge eternal, we revere you.
Father eternal, we love you.
God eternal, we adore you,
*   we praise you,*
*   we thank you.*

You have come to us, and now we respond to you
*   expectantly, for you will not withhold what your children need;*
*   trustingly, for we can count upon your constancy;*
*   eagerly, for we know we are meant for you;*
*   thankfully, for your mercies endure forever.*

We look to you now to penetrate and permeate all of life with
your Spirit, for your Spirit alone can renew and refresh and
refine. Then grant us
*   the integrity which reflects our Lord's single-mindedness,*
*   the gentleness which reflects his approach to bruised*
*   people,*
*   the resilience which reflects his resistance to the evil one,*
*   the self-forgetfulness which will risk all for his kingdom*
*   only to be surprised at finding all in his presence.*

In our moments of discouragement,
In the world's moments of cynicism,
In the church's moments of hesitation,
Surge over us once more and we shall declare from our hearts

that life can begin again, for in our midst
the habituated have found release,
the embittered have found a new mind,
the caustic have found a new tongue, and
the unbelieving have found their God.

As often as we recognize the world's deepest hunger,
As often as we see its attempt at easing it,
As often as we hear our Lord's "I AM,"
So let us hold up him whose shed blood will ever be
its life,
its hope, and
its happiness.

*We pray in the confidence that who you are for us you are
eternally. Amen.*

DAY 7

A Woman at a Well (1)
John 4:5-26, 39-42.

"What's so fortunate about having oil?" the Arab leader asked the startled North Americans; "You people have rain." He was correct. Rain is infinitely more precious than a non-replenishable supply of oil. It takes only one thing for the desert to blossom like a rose: water. Water is life. For good reason Jesus speaks of himself as "living water." He alone quenches life's profoundest thirst.

The early church exulted in the one who was life-giving water and who therefore imparted fruitfulness to human existence. Peter writes to Christian friends, "You believe in him with unutterable and exalted joy." Paul cries, "He loved me, and gave himself for *me!*" John exclaims, "We know that we have passed out of death into life." And the unknown author of Hebrews insists, "We have tasted the powers of the age to come."

Let's not deceive ourselves: people do have a life-thirst; they do long for that of which the apostles speak. And just as certainly they expect the church to be acquainted with this water and to be a conduit for it. Where we fail to point to the thirst-quenching one their disappointment and anguish stare at us. Margaret Anderson, a British poet writes:

> O preacher, holy man, hear my heart weeping;
> I long to stand and shout my protests:
> Where is your power? And where is your message?
> Where is the gospel of mercy and love?
> Your words are nothingness! nothingness!
>   nothingness!
> We who have come to listen are betrayed.
> Servant of God, I am bitter and desolate.

What do I care for perfection of phrase?
Cursed be your humour, your poise, your diction.
See how my soul turns to ashes within me.
You who have vowed to declare your Redeemer
Give me the words that would save.
("A Wail from a Distressed Soul", quoted in L.
Weatherhead's *The Christian Agnostic*, p.2)

On one occasion another needy woman met Jesus at a well. She assumed that he was thirsty too. It's no wonder, then, she was surprised to see him standing there without a bucket. How did he think he was ever going to draw water? Jesus said to her, "If you knew who I am and what I give, you would be asking me for a drink. If you drink the water that I give, you will never thirst again."

Christians know that Jesus Christ can assuage life's thirsts. For it's our experience that water is enough to make what's arid fertile.

Prayer

Gracious God, through your prophet you told us that water would break forth in the wilderness and streams in the desert. You have fulfilled your word in Jesus Christ our Lord. We praise you today that the water of life which you are is given to us in him.

We come to you admitting our thirst, for the sieves we thought would hold water are sieves indeed:
> *pleasure which cloys,*
> *busyness which bores,*
> *entertainment which only distracts, and*
> *experimentation which jades.*
Yet we rejoice that in Jesus Christ you have come upon us as showers come upon thirsty land:
> *moistening what is parched,*
> *softening what is hard,*

invigorating what is infertile, and
making fruitful what is barren.

We praise you for this woman
  whose boldness was greater than her shame, and
  whose audacity overcame years of ingrained custom, and
  whose eagerness exceeded her natural reluctance.
For we, like her, must reach out beyond convention to meet
      our Lord;
    we, like her, must hear the Master pronounce the truth
      about us which we do not like but should not deny;
    we, like her, must know that he seals off escape routes only
      because he wants to do in us more than we ask or
      think; and then
    we, like her, shall exult as he receives us,
                  nourishes us and
                  cheers us.
Again let your living water
  come upon us,
  course through us,
  spill over us,
and then let our neighbours, like hers, believe on our Lord
      because of our word.

We pray to you now knowing you are that pool
  from whom we can draw,
  of whom we can drink,
  unto whom we must return as surely as the
      rivers find their way to the sea. Amen.

DAY 8

A Woman at a Well
(The Samaritan Woman)(2)
John 4:5-26, 39-42

The conversation at the well doesn't continue forever. Jesus stalls it with one remark: "Why don't you get your husband and bring him here?" Cautious, now, the woman replies, "I don't have a husband." "I know that you haven't," adds the Master gently, "You've had five, and the man you are living with now isn't your husband."

All of us can (and do) play games with Jesus Christ—until his question or comment stalls our cleverly contrived evasion. His remark needn't pertain to the moral aspect of our lives (as it did with her); it can pertain to any aspect. In fact he directs his remark to that area of our lives where it is most likely to bring us up short, most likely to shatter our illusion of self-sufficiency and complacency. He speaks to us precisely where moisture is so lacking that the desert of our existence hasn't blossomed as a rose. C.S. Lewis, for instance, learned that the profound, nameless longing which had haunted him for years was the remark the Master was addressing to him. Those who enjoy the endless subtlety of religious speculation one day overhear him saying, "Why don't you just admit that you are trying to avoid me?" Or on another day we admit, however reluctantly, that the things with which we have cluttered our lives haven't rendered us one whit happier. Perhaps we become honest enough with ourselves to admit that our besetting temptation has such a deadly grip on us because we secretly enjoy it. These "discernments" are merely the converse side of his question or comment. There is simply no end to the ways our Lord can effectively thwart our trifling with him.

In all of this we mustn't think that he brings us up short

primarily in order to cause discomfort, promote anxiety or create guilt. He does it in order to remove the smoke screens which hide us from him. He does it to create receptivity for the living water which he is and which he pours out upon us.

Prayer

Eternal God, your word is sharper than a two-edged sword and alone discerns the thoughts and intentions of the heart. We do not pretend anything else, for repeatedly your truth has pierced us through and through. Today we praise you that you penetrate us only to remove what is unsightly, what is unseemly, and what inhibits our growth as your sons and daughters.

>   *If we find your severity harsh, remind us that it serves*
>   *your kindness.*
>   *If we find your judgement onerous, remind us that it serves*
>   *your mercy.*
>   *If we find your anger hot, remind us that it serves the balm*
>   *of your love.*

As we read of our Lord's exposure of the Samaritan woman, save us from thinking ourselves less sinful than she, or more holy, or superior in any way.
For with unnerving stare our Lord
>   *sees past our screens,*
>   *brushes aside our excuses, and*
>   *ignores our defences as he accosts us:*
>   *"Go call your alienated child"*
>   *"Produce your income tax return"*
>   *"Show me the lonely person for whom you gave up leisure*
>   *time"*
>   *"Bring back the person your tongue*
>   *slew."*
And like her, we are driven to say, "I can't."

Then let us receive from our Lord

the touch that heals,
the word that pardons,
the look that lifts up,
the smile that blesses.

And turn us out of ourselves as our new life in him directs us
to a world awaiting our witness,
to people whose pain needs relieving,
to an earth whose groan is unceasing.

Move us to begin and end the day with you, our God, for you will
ever surround us in truth, in love, and in peace. Amen.

DAY 9

A Woman At a Well
(The Samaritan Woman)(3)
John 4:5-26, 39-42

Turned around by her encounter with Jesus the woman blurts out her story to the townspeople. Through her testimony many of them come to the same conviction and confession. They say to her, "It is no longer because of your words that we believe, for we have heard for ourselves and we know that this is indeed the Saviour of the World."

The ring of assurance is unmistakable: "for ourselves...we know." Assurance is indeed an aspect of faith. The expression "we know" occurs fifteen times in 1 John, an epistle only a few pages long. When church dignitaries upbraided John Wesley for the supposed presumptuousness of assurance, telling him that his enthusiasm was in poor taste, Wesley replied quietly, "Can a person be a child of God and not know it?"

Of course there's a pseudo-certainty born of wicked prejudice. And regardless of the prejudice—racial, ethnic, economic, religious, educational, social—the more ridiculous the prejudice the greater is the "conviction" and the certainty of those who cloak themselves in it. But all such pseudo-certainty ought not to blind us to the life-significance of being moved to say with the Samaritan townspeople, "It is no longer because of your words that we believe, for we have heard for ourselves and we know...." For faith is neither wistfulness nor wishful thinking nor hoping for the best. Faith is a distinctive knowing that arises from our Lord's having met us and addressed us, seized us and saved us.

In 1563 the Reformed Church produced the *Heidelberg Catechism*. It was intended for the Christian education of adults. It has worn well and we creatures of modernity can learn much from it. Its first question is, "What is your only comfort in life and in death?" Answer: "My only comfort in life and in death is that I am not my own but I belong, body and soul, to my faithful Saviour Jesus Christ." Jesus insists that he is the Good Shepherd, and then adds, "I know my own and *my own know me.*" The Samaritan woman knew. And because she did many others came to know as well.

Prayer

Gracious God, you call men and women today just as you called Abraham and Sarah, Isaac and Rebecca, Jacob and Rachel. You call us today as you called your people in the earthly ministry of Jesus our Lord. We thank you that you have called us by name, that your call has created in us and elicited from us the response heard from Samuel,

"Speak, Lord, for your servant hears,"
as well as that heard from Isaiah,
"Here am I, send me."

We listen anew today for you, knowing that you will confirm in us your summons to keep company with our Lord.
Let that summons sound forth
clearly in the midst of competing sounds,
challengingly in the midst of attractive palliatives,
convincingly in the midst of our hesitations,
compellingly in the midst of our inertia.

Remind us that we must not expect another's call to resemble ours, for there is no end to the ways you invite people to become disciples: the clear word of a sermon,
the haunting word of a hymn,
the startling word of someone's rebuke,
the persistent word of a mother's devotion.
Because we are creatures marred by the Fall, we know we can confuse "religious conviction" with cherished prejudices. Then ever

remake us in mind and spirit, loosening the grip of
  our secret insecurities,
  our petty grievances,
  our festering wounds,
  our frustrated ambitions.

*Give us the assurance that we are yours inasmuch as we do in
fact belong to you, for indeed*
  your hold on us is tighter than our hold on you,
  your love for us greater than our love for you, and
  your mercy vaster than our sin.

*We look to you at this time, confident that you are worthy of our
trust and our love. For in Jesus Christ you have stood by us and
will stand with us for ever and ever. Amen.*

DAY 10

A Fragmented Fellow (1)
Mark 5:1-20

His name was "legion." He was a jumble of "selves." We know how he felt. We too know the daily pressure to be *this* to one person, *that* to another person, and something else again in another situation. We keep shuffling the false faces, telling ourselves that we do have to survive in this world, after all. But one day we start to feel that we are nothing more than the shuffling of the false faces. And we are scared.

Or we compromise ourselves seriously. At first we insist that the compromise doesn't really affect us since we are at least aware of the inner contradiction. But soon the compromise bites so deep that we ourselves become the lie—even the lies. We find that we can't distinguish ourselves from the falsehoods and phoniness that have overtaken us. And we are scared.

As soon as we suspect that someone is "seeing through" us, our fragile ego is exposed and fragmentation intensifies. If others now pronounce us "legion" we feel threatened with extinction. Any creature so threatened flies into hostility. While we are quick to label the hostile person as "just mean," a look inside ourselves tells us that most hostility arises from fear; fear that our "legion" condition is evident to everyone, fear that we don't know who we really are.

Jesus heals the fellow in Mark's story—which is to say, in Jesus Christ the fellow finds his real self. Now he has an identity: a disciple of the one through whom and for whom all things have been made. Little wonder the townspeople find him seated, clothed, and in his right mind. No longer frenzied or legion-minded he feels unthreatened as his hostility evaporates.

No doubt many voices continued to whisper to the fellow, just as the same voices whisper falsehoods to us, chief of which is that we don't belong to the one who has created, called and healed us. But these voices are silenced by that greater voice, says Isaiah, who insists, "I have called you by name; you are mine."

Prayer

Gracious God, with all Israel we look to you and cry: "The Lord our God is one Lord." We praise you that before all the pseudo-deities which clamour for our attention and compete for our allegiance, you continue to stamp yourself upon us as the one God, Sovereign and Saviour, whom we are to hear and heed in life and in death.

We confess that pressures upon us from without often divide us from within, and we say one thing to someone in one situation, something else to someone in another, and something else again when we feel critical eyes are upon us or our acceptability is in question or promotion is at stake.

We know in our hearts that to shuffle false faces can only mean that one day we shall not know who we are and shall not be able to be trusted. Then as we dread this development within us, touch our fear with your grace, that our fear might awaken us to our need of healing, and might move us to welcome your work of restoration.

Keep us looking unto Jesus, for
> *it is he who seats us—as at last our fragmentation is under control;*
> *it is he who clothes us—as we know we belong to him and his people;*
> *it is he who restores us to our right mind-- as we repudiate the folly that wants to recapture us.*

*Increase our awareness of fragmented people around us, especially
those who have been broken by the chaos in our world:*
> *the unemployed person whose self-confidence is crumbling
> day by day;*
> *the worker in the arms industry who agonizes over the
> manufacture of death;*
> *the business person who can no longer hide the shortfall
> from the shareholders;*
> *the environmentalist who is near-frantic over the ravages
> of nature's degradation.*
*For all such people we intercede at this time, trusting you to let
them see their wholeness in Christ, asking you to help us reflect
this truth to those whose lips are forming "legion."*

*Come upon us afresh, we plead, that as you visit us, speak to us
and touch us you will suppress that chaos without which
threatens to move within.*

*We look to you, our God, for you alone are the rightful ruler and
redeemer of us all. Amen.*

DAY 11

A Fragmented Fellow (2)
Mark 5:1-20.

Following the restoration of the fellow mentioned yesterday we should expect a street party in the town. For who could object to the recovery of someone whose life would otherwise have remained painful, dangerous and useless? Yet the townspeople "begged Jesus to depart." Really, we shouldn't be surprised. They have seen that Jesus can expose evil readily and operate on it drastically. Then what might he expose about them? How uncomfortable, even costly, might it be to have him around? He is clearly someone to be reckoned with. He can't be controlled. They can only tell him to disappear.

It's easy to see why Christians are persecuted relentlessly in any totalitarian state. In one sense oddly, in another sense understandably, a few people who gather to sing, pray and preach manage to menace a world power. For here are people who have gained their identity and right-mindedness through Jesus Christ and who can pretend nothing else. Knowing who they are in him, they can't be hoodwinked or manipulated by strong-arm ideology; neither can they be cowed by its brutality. As expected they have the same effect on their government as the restored man had on his neighbours: Jesus Christ must be expelled. In the same way Christians in Stalin's Soviet Republics, in Hitler's Germany, in Pot Pol's Cambodia, in Zedong's China, and in so many countries of Latin America ultimately prove impervious to the poison of the political tyrants and military oppressors and economic exploiters who twist and torment and brainwash.

We must be careful, of course, in discussing the rejection accorded Jesus by authoritarian regimes. For we can also dismiss him ourselves, albeit more subtly. Dietrich Bonhoeffer

---

maintained that it's the pseudo-disciple, faced with the foolishness and weakness and sin of the church, who can always find a reason that "explains" it and someone to blame for it. But the true disciple can only say, together with those who sat at supper with Jesus, "Lord, is it I?" If ever we think we are beyond having to ask, "Lord, is it I?", then we too have begged the Master to depart. Beg as we might in our folly and defensiveness, his glorious promise is that he won't forsake us or fail us.

Prayer

Eternal God,
   your constancy constrains us to cast ourselves upon you;
   your love impels us to trust you;
   your mercy moves us to repent before you; while
   your joy cheers us and dispels the gloom which
      would otherwise oppress us.

We praise you that your name, for which Moses asked, you have spelled for us in Jesus of Nazareth. Then fix our gaze upon him, for in seeing him we shall see you who have given him to us.

As we think upon the man whom our Lord healed, as well as those whom he heals today, we pray for those who have become the target of the world's hostility. For it is as Christ's people inevitably point to him that he and they are asked to depart. So it is we lift up before you for your blessing
   those in North Korea who will not renounce their Lord;
   those in Africa who see him violated in the violation of
      their neighbour;
   those in China who have kept the flame of faith alive;
   those in North America whose peacemaking is labelled
      treasonous.

And as the apostles have commanded us to do, we intercede today for rulers everywhere:

*for the rulers of the superpowers whose hands hold weapons
        beyond our imagining;*
*for the rulers of developing countries who ought not to ignore
        the pain of their malnourished citizens;*
*for the rulers of our own nation who are struggling to hold
        together a country whose history has left bitterness;*
*for the rulers of municipalities who must contend with
        toxic waste and abused children and asphalted
        farmland.*

*As we reflect on the reception accorded our Lord throughout his
creation we know we are prone to expel him ourselves. Then
convict and convince us afresh, we ask, that our Lord's work in us
will be like a city set on a hill: unmistakable and undeniable.*

*We thank you that we find ourselves made whole and seen to be
whole in the Son with whom you are ever pleased. Amen.*

DAY 12

ZACCHAEUS (1)
Luke 19:1-10

Fire attracts animals. Yet fire also keeps animals at bay. The animal is intrigued by fire and approaches it. Yet the animal is also made apprehensive by fire and keeps its distance from it. Many people react to Jesus Christ in the same way. He attracts them, and they begin to approach him. At the same time they are wary of coming too close. Zacchaeus was like this. He had heard much about Jesus, found himself intrigued, and decided he had to see Jesus for himself. The tree-perch was the perfect place for him. He would be close enough to see Jesus for himself, yet far enough away to be out of reach; close enough to "get a line on" Jesus, distant enough to be safe. Curious he was; committed he was not. He didn't want to be hassled or embarrassed in any way. The tree-perch was perfect.

Don't we all know people like the little man? They want a perspective from which they can see life whole, a point around which life is integrated, a centre whose circumference determines the "boundaries" of their existence. Yet they are suspicious of religious eccentricity. Pious "hype" puts them off.

They are also looking for resources. While they couldn't turn up the Bible verse which speaks of those who "have the form of religion but deny the power of it," they are certainly aware of the distinction. The "power of it" they are looking for; the "form of it" they are not. They want help. But they also want to appear "cool." "No sweat" is how they like to speak of themselves.

The same people are looking for a foundational certainty; the certainty that God is, that God cares, that God makes a significant difference to life. Yet they can't stand the "certainty" of propaganda or the "conviction" of those who won't think.

Nevertheless they crave inner assurance of the truth and reality of God. They suspect that Jesus is somehow related to it. The tree-perch is the perfect vantage point: they can see what Jesus is all about while avoiding contact with those whose zeal for him puts them off.

Prayer

Gracious God, men and women whom you call and invigorate have always found in your Son, Jesus, that shepherd whom they must name "good." We too have found him not only upright but also winsome, appealing, attractive. We praise you that he reflects your glory and bears the stamp of your nature. Clarify our vision of him, we ask, that we might be drawn to him afresh, and being drawn to him, might know with greater certainty you who have given him to us and us to him.

We intercede today for all manner of people who are attracted to our Lord in any way:
    those who are intrigued by a teaching they cannot forget;
    those who are won by his love for the poor;
    those who admire his single-mindedness unto death;
    those who are moved by his forgiving his enemies;
    those who have turned to him when others failed to perform
        what they had promised.
Continue to move within all such people that they might at last find their longing satisfied in our Lord,
    their hope grounded in his victory,
    their trust confirmed again and again.

We who take the name of Jesus upon our lips and who are therefore an advertisement for him, pray that
    you will invigorate us with your Spirit until we glow with
        warmth and light;
    you will defuse our anxiety until we are transparent to him
        who says, "Fear not;"
    you will enlarge our generosity until we give as he gave—

without reserve;
you will quicken our compassion until we are moved by a
heart that aches.

It is to you, O God, that we look at all times and in all
circumstances, for it is you who have
created us in love,
redeemed us in mercy,
called us by the truth, and
summon us now to follow him in whom is found everything
you wish us to be and do.

Then let our praise of you begin and end the day, for you are
indeed worthy to be praised. Amen.

DAY 13

ZACCHAEUS (2)
Luke 19:1-10

Jesus stops at the foot of the tree, looks up and says, "What on earth are you doing up there? Come on down. I'm going to your house. We're going to eat." If Jesus had said, "Get off that silly perch," Zacchaeus might still be there. Who doesn't stiffen when told in such a manner as to be "told off?" What brings Zacchaeus out of the tree is our Lord's insistence that he is going to eat on the little man's "turf," in his house.

Eating was a sign of the most intimate friendship. To have a meal with someone meant that you accepted that person without condition. No hidden agenda was going to emerge halfway through the meal. The shared meal was a pact of peace, forgiveness and solidarity. Then it's no surprise the gospel writers show us Jesus eating again and again, no surprise so many of his parables have to do with food. The shared meal was the sign of exile ended, of elevation to honour, of rehabilitation.

Only Christ's limitless mercy, forgiveness, kindness; only his free acceptance frees people from their defensiveness and moves them to abandon their tree-perch. Magnifying their shortcomings won't do it. This merely humiliates them. Sending them on guilt-trips won't do it. This makes them either self-righteous or neurotic. We should note that Zacchaeus's bad reputation—entirely deserved—Jesus doesn't even mention. He knows what Zacchaeus has been about for years, yet says nothing about it at this time. Tree-perchers aren't persuaded to abandon their roost through being harangued or threatened, nor by being reminded, subtly or not so subtly, of the defects about them which they and others can see only too plainly. They abandon their perch only as they find in the approach of Jesus Christ an acceptance, a pardon and a joy which melts their suspicion and lifts their head.

Prayer

Eternal God, it is as we think upon the wisdom and kindness of our Lord Jesus Christ that we lift head and heart and voice and cry, "Thanks be to you for your unspeakable gift." For it is the gift which is the giver himself that startles us as we recall
the worth your gift confers on us,
the joy your gift engenders within us,
the task to which your gift points us.

Hear us this day as our worship ascends to you, for you, of your grace, have spoken to us, and we, of our gratitude, must speak now to you.

As we think upon the man whom our Lord neither disdained nor passed by, we are awakened afresh to his mercy:
that mercy which is rooted in the tender heart of you the pardoning one;
that mercy which is love poured out on those who are doomed without it;
that mercy which is pardon visited upon those who never deserve it;
that mercy which cleanses us when we are soiled and clears us when we are accused.

Then let us all, in company with the apostle, say with heartfelt thanksgiving, "I received mercy." And then let us live for you whose mercy has brought life to us.

As you continue to work in us a new heart, a new mind and a new spirit, stifle
the vengeance in us that nurses an injury,
the unforgiving heart that remembers an old wound,

*the unkindness that is content to meet hostility with
    indifference.*

*Let our mercy flow over
    any whose word has cut us,
    any whose slander has defamed us,
    any whose cunning has exploited us,
    any whose betrayal has victimized us.*

*We thank you today for the meals you share with us and at
which you share yourself:
    the Eucharist which renews your work in us and confirms
        our life in you;
    the church supper which fosters friendship and cements
        community;
    the daily meals in homes which you grace now just as you
        graced meal tables in your earthly ministry.*

*As we return to our work in your world, grant that this time of
devotion will bear fruit for us, for others, and for all who long to
see the kingdoms of this earth become the kingdom of our God.
Amen.*

DAY 14

ZACCHAEUS (3)
Luke 19:1-10 (3)

And then there was the big giveaway. With his feet on solid ground Zacchaeus couldn't help saying, "Here and now I give away half my possessions. And anyone I have cheated I am ready to repay four times over." His turned-around outlook was a spontaneous outflowing of his delight in his new friend. He didn't have to have his arm twisted; Jesus didn't have to lean on him. The mood was joyful gratitude as Zacchaeus gladly did what he knew a disciple should do.

When I was a youngster my mother would ask me to rake leaves or shovel snow or cut grass. I would do it all right—but do it grudgingly. She would become exasperated and gasp, "I'm asking you to do only one little thing. Why do you have to look so hard done by?" Under my breath I would mutter, "You wanted the leaves raked; you're getting the leaves raked. So what's your objection?" Now I understand her objection and her upset. A claim upon us which we don't meet cheerfully, gladly, willingly is simply not met at all. Haven't you asked someone to give you a hand with some undertaking only to find that he did it so grudgingly you wished you had never asked him? Martin Luther never wearied of reminding us that an obedience which isn't glad and joyful is no obedience at all. When next we teach a Sunday School class, drive a patient on behalf of the Cancer Society, assist someone who, for now, can only receive while we can only give, or sit through church meetings that are less than thrilling but without which there would be no Christian presence in the community at all—on such occasions we must see this truth.

We know we aren't going to be (and aren't expected to be) flying from one "high" to another all day, every day. Yet to know that Jesus has eaten with us is to know that real obedience is glad obedience. It's to be grateful for the privilege of serving Jesus Christ in a world of deprivation and suffering. As Zacchaeus climbed out of his perch he knew himself impelled and freed to spend himself gladly for any and all, without hesitation, reservation or qualification.

Prayer

Father of our Lord Jesus Christ, we approach you today because
you have first approached us;
you have caused us to hear you;
you have warmed our cold hearts and freed our frozen
tongues.
Receive our worship, we pray, for we want again to declare your
worthiness as we adore you anew.

Illumine for us our Lord Jesus, that we might see afresh his
generosity, and seeing it, find his Spirit quickening ours.
Immersed as we are in a world bent on acquiring things,
hoarding things,
displaying things,
flaunting things,
we know we are subtly edged towards acquisitiveness,
effectively made grasping,
persistently urged to rationalize it all.
Free us from our possessions lest we become possessed by them as
surely as evil spirits possessed others. And just as our Lord
healed those whom the demons afflicted, grant us deliverance
from the toys and trinkets and trifles that blunt our zeal and
stifle our sacrifice.

In a world where so many have so little, we live as the few with
so much. Then help us to be stewards of what you have entrusted
to us:
fresh air and water,
forest and farmland,

minerals and money.

Fortify our obedience that we might share out of ourselves
whatever will sustain the needy. Grant that
  our cheerfulness will meet their sadness,
  our hospitality will dispel their loneliness,
  our listening will defuse their frustration, and
  our intercession will offer the prayer they can't quite utter.

In all of this let our joy be irrepressible,
              our humour infectious,
              our obedience glad, and
              our open-handedness without guile.
For we follow gladly him whose commandments are not
                            burdensome,
              whose service is our freedom, and
              whose summons is our peace.

Grant that our friendship with him who sticks closer than a
brother will move us
  to let go what we clutch,
  to share what we hold, and
  to thank you, our God, for calling us to him who gives without
      measure and without end. Amen.

DAY 15

PETER (1)
Matthew 16:13-20

Was he really a "rock", as Jesus nicknamed him, or was our Lord merely joking, the way we joke when we call a fat person "slim?" Let's wait and see. In any case, Jesus did call Peter to be a disciple. Thereafter Peter was regarded as the spokesperson for all disciples of his era and of any era after his.

Today we who are disciples assent to Peter's great affirmation of faith: "You are the Christ, the son of the living God. You are the very presence and power and purpose of God." This apparently narrow acknowledgement grates on many people. Surely it's an exaggeration, if not outright arrogance, to speak of God so very precisely. Isn't God more diffuse than this? Yet the effectiveness of a knife depends on the precision of its cutting edge. A youngster who wants to burn his initials into a park bench knows that the power of the sun is too diffuse to do anything. A magnifying glass focuses the sun's rays at one pinpoint. Now there's a concentrated intensity which can do something. In Jesus Christ God concentrates himself to a pinpoint intensity which allows us to recognize him, acknowledge him, ally ourselves with him and announce what he is doing.

To say this is not to say that we "know it all." But knowing Christ as the pinpoint intensity of God we can do something besides shrug our shoulders when our child asks us about the faith. It won't settle the matter of career ("Should I be an accountant or a nurse?"), but it will settle the matter of vocation, for vocation is reflecting the discernment, compassion and integrity of Jesus Christ wherever we earn a living. It doesn't give us a formula or a cure-all for handling relentless evil and ceaseless suffering. But it does undo paralysis in the face of these, for in Christ God has overcome our world of tribulation and summons us to give visibility to his victory.

When Peter cries, "You are the Christ!", he is saying everything about God we have mentioned above. Yet he is saying much about us as well. While he and we have certainly not "arrived" we do know we have stopped groping for the road.

Prayer

Eternal God, your word is
  a rock which can withstand any assault,
  a shower which refreshes the weary sojourner,
  a cloud through which your glory shines, and
  clothing which we, your people, are to put on and wear
      forever.

We thank you today
  that you always send forth your word,
  that it always achieves the purpose for which you send it,
  that its goodness we have tasted ourselves
      and now know what you have in store for us.

Together with all in your community we rejoice that
  you call us, by name, to become disciples;
  you summon us, each one, to keep following our Lord;
  you give us, without exception, what we need for the living
      of our days;
  you encourage us, again and again, to hold fast to him
      whose grip on us will secure us forever.

As the light which you are is focused in Jesus our Lord, only to stream from him to us and our world, let that light enlighten our hearts and illumine our path.
Give us a spirit of discernment that we might see what you
      want of us,

a spirit of obedience that we might hasten to do it,
a spirit of joy that your command might be our delight,
a spirit of contentment that dispels our grumbling.

While we do not pretend to have arrived at our journey's end, or to be the spiritual giant we are not, we do know that our Lord himself is the way even as he accompanies us on it.

Then grant us humility, that we shall learn of him who can help us,
love, that we shall welcome diverse fellow travellers,
peace, that in all things we shall commend him who brings peace.

For you are our God, and you will keep us yours forever. Amen.

DAY 16

PETER (2)
Mark 14:66-72

In Peter's faltering discipleship we see reflected our own fumbling, stumbling, falling-down discipleship. Too quickly we insist, "I shall never let you down. You can count on *me*." One day later it took only a fifteen-year-old domestic to crumble the rugged fisherman: "Your accent: you sound just like that other fellow who's soon going to get it in the neck." As Peter looses a torrent of oaths and obscenities he hears the rooster again. And the tears stream down his face like water pouring down the side of a rock.

We are disciples too. Yet we remember the time we erupted with a put-down so savage that we shocked ourselves as we whipped the skin off someone else. It came out so fast it seemed natural. Yet it isn't supposed to be natural to disciples. We recall the time someone had found us out concerning something we didn't want publicized. We lied, and in a few seconds had to lie again. We began to wonder if there is anything to us besides falsehood. You remember that business trip where something besides business was carried on, and only two days later you had to teach Sunday school. You felt as though someone had taken a pneumatic drill to your stomach. Or we fell down badly in front of our children. Stupidly thinking it virtuous to save face, and still more stupidly thinking we could save face, we tried to excuse the inexcusable and succeeded only in making dishonest fools of ourselves before our children. Stunned, we said to ourselves, "But I'm supposed to be a disciple." And like Peter we wept bitterly. (If we didn't, then we have turned a deaf ear to the rooster's cry.)

It is a sign of our Lord's mercy that he continues to name us his disciples. As we find our compromised discipleship mirrored in Peter's, we know afresh that it is by grace, by grace alone, that we are Christ's forever.

Prayer

Eternal God, the Psalmist tells us that from the rising of the sun to its setting, your name is to be praised. And just as he felt you weighing upon him, we too know you are pressing yourself upon us, impressing yourself upon us, that we might be marked as your people, praising you for as long as we have breath.

We rejoice that we are your "peculiar treasure," those whom you have called and equipped as servants and instruments for the sake of those whom you will add to your people.

Even as we are your people, however, we cannot deny that
*   our discipleship is inconsistent,*
*   our devotion is spasmodic,*
*   our obedience is fitful, and*
*   our faithfulness is intermittent.*

Like Peter we hear the rooster crow.
Like Peter we pretend that what is evident to everyone else cannot be true for us—for we are Christians:
*   we are the twice born;*
*   we have passed from death to life.*

Then your servant Luther reminds us that the "old" man or woman is dead, yet the corpse still twitches. Even as remorse sweeps over us, save us from wallowing. As our self-confidence is shaken, save us from despair. For despite our fumbling and stumbling we do long to be Christ's people,
*   we do aim at obeying him,*
*   we do want to live in love and truth and integrity.*

*As the assurance of our pardon settles upon us anew, use the
occasion to increase our understanding of those who have
stumbled as we have,
to temper our judgment of those who
don't measure up,
to strengthen our ties with those who have let us down,
to magnify the mercy we must extend to others.*

*At the beginning of the day and at its ending, let us know that it
is grace, and only grace, which has called us,
renewed us,
sustained us, and
elicited our praise of you our
God who alone are our
glory. Amen.*

DAY 17

PETER (3)

John 21:15-17

Peter represents us in the use our Lord makes of us and will ever make of us. Three times (once for each denial) Jesus asks, "Do you love me?" Three times Peter replies soberly, "You know that I love you." And three times Jesus commissions him, "Feed my sheep." Peter's stumbling hasn't disqualified him. He is entrusted with nurturing other disciples and would-be disciples in the Christian community. He's been given a responsibility that he alone can fulfill.

Our Lord entrusts us too with a task on behalf of his people. If we protest that our discipleship isn't of such sterling sort as to qualify us for his service, he will interrupt us mid-sentence, saying, "I ask only, do you love me?" Of course people take spills. Often the spills are disgraceful; they are always a denial of Jesus and a contradiction of our discipleship. But no spill renders anyone of no use to God and no significance before God. If defective discipleship disqualified us then the Good Shepherd would have no one whom he could use in his shepherding. But he does have "shepherds" without number, for he asks of us only, "Do you love me?"—and then sends us to do his work among his people.

So esteemed became Peter's reputation as a Christian leader that the people of Jerusalem laid their sick friends in the street that his shadow might fall on them. The Jerusalem people knew of Peter's weakness and inconsistency. They knew also of his large-hearted love for Jesus. And this carried more weight with them than anything else.

We must return to the question we didn't answer: was Jesus merely joking when he called Peter "rocky?" The practice of naming was so important to Jews that they never joked about it. Jesus meant exactly what he said. The rock is Peter himself, together with his acknowledgement that Jesus Christ is the effectual presence of God, plus his large-hearted love for his Lord. Despite the weaknesses in our discipleship, the same Lord says as much to us: we are rocks, stones, even "living stones" with which he will build that church that not even the powers of death and destruction can threaten (1 Peter 2:5).

Prayer

Gracious God, the apostle John insists that you are love. Such love is too deep for us to comprehend,
  too rich for us to appreciate fully,
  too vast for us to measure.
Yet this very love you invite us to drink up,
      plunge into,
      bathe in,
for this love surrounds us and supports your world.

In the midst of all that contradicts it, and especially when we, your people, contradict it, let us hear our Lord, your love incarnate, asking us once more, "Do you love me?"

So magnify his voice that we shall hear it more distinctly and more persuasively than we hear
 the voice of self-rejection which whispers that we cannot
  love him,
 the voice of guilt which reminds us that we are flawed
  followers,
 the voice of anxiety which tells us we don't really trust
  him,
 the voice of petulance which faults him for our pain.

As we hear him ask, "Do you love me?", give us grace to respond in voice and heart as he longs to hear us respond: "You know that I love you."

*Increase our love for our Lord, we ask, for in loving him we shall
love his people who are included in him:*

   the fellow parishioner who disagrees with us so often,
   *the elderly relative whose short memory and shorter
           temper irk us unspeakably,*
   *the young schizophrenic whom someone must support for
           the rest of her life,*
   *the adolescent whose insecurity seems to require more love and
           more patience than we have to give.*

*Gracious God, you ask us only to love all such for Christ's sake.
Then enlarge our vision of him until we can see his arms around
all whom we find loving a challenge.*

*In our turbulent days, when principalities and powers assail our
Christian conviction and confession, give us each to know again
that all disciples are "rock," for you have embedded us in him who
is the cornerstone, and him you have raised triumphant over
death.*

*It is to you, eternal God, to whom we ascribe all praise and glory
and honour. Amen.*

DAY 18

BARTIMAEUS (1)
Mark 10: 46-52

Do we become disciples only when we've achieved a measure of theological sophistication? From our Lord's encounter with Bartimaeus we know that to be a disciple is always to be a disciple-in-the-making, always to be in the process of being formed and informed by Jesus. The truth is, we can begin our discipleship as simply as did Bartimaeus: with the simple admission that we are blind and poor. We lack enlightenment and we lack resources. The blind fellow doesn't address Jesus by any of the "advanced" titles, such as Son of God, Saviour, or Lord. He surmises that Jesus is somehow related to Israel's greatest king, and having heard that the Nazarene is in the neighbourhood, he calls out, "Son of David, help me."

Surely discipleship begins this way for most of us. We recognize the dark areas and the impoverishment of our lives; we simply ask for help. Discipleship begins before, sometimes a long time before, we can hang the correct labels on Jesus. Like Bartimaeus, of course, we must persist with our plea even in the face of an unsympathetic crowd which tells him to be silent. As fledgling disciples, we must want what we are looking for so badly that we can taste it. We must want it enough to persist despite others' scorn or belittlement or apathy. We can't be deflected by those who maintain that Jesus has been dead for two thousand years, that faith is merely a crutch for the immature and the inept, or that discipleship is a throwback to killjoy Victorianism. Bartimaeus heard it all, yet called out more persistently.

Discipleship is, in truth, both more simple and more difficult than many imagine. It's simpler because our mere acknowledgement of our need and of Christ's availability will render us disciples-in-the-making; more difficult because we must persist despite detractors. Bartimaeus craved insight for his blindness and resources for his poverty. His craving was enough to stop Jesus in his tracks and say, "Call that fellow."

Prayer

Eternal God, the Psalmist knows that you have been the dwelling-place of your people for all generations. We have come to know this for ourselves.

Today we praise you that you are the one
from whom we have come,
to whom we go,
under whom we live, and
in whom we rest ourselves.

As we ponder again your presence and power and purpose, increase our confidence that your everlasting arms support us, just as they supported our foreparents in faith and will support our descendants as well.

We thank you that in Christ Jesus you meet us and speak to us and receive us, even when our understanding of you is imperfect and our acquaintance with you seems slight:
when we are confused, yet wonder whether you might have light to shed upon us;
when we are bereft and doubt whether there is someone who can console us;
when we are guilty and want a pardon as deep as our disquiet;
when we are agitated and need the peace that only the truth can bring.

We ask you to strengthen our discipleship day by day, for our weakness has exposed our constant need of grace.
Fortify our loyalty when false gods lure us.

Increase our faith when tragedy blunts our trust.
Enlarge our love when rebuff and reproach prick us.
Refresh our hope when the tyrants of the world drive us to
> *cry, "How long?"*

We intercede for disciples of our Lord around the world who are
tempted to desert him. We plead an infusion of your
encouragement and joy
> *for those who struggle for human rights in a country which*
>> *tramples them;*
> *for those who have protested bomb-making only to be*
>> *called "traitor;"*
> *for those who have sided with the dispossessed only to find*
>> *other Christians uncomprehending;*
> *for those who have wrestled with their besetting sin and*
>> *are determined never to yield.*

Grant to all such people
> *a clear vision of their Lord who is on the road with them;*
> *a heightened hearing of him whose call will never be revoked;*
> *a single-minded obedience to him whose service is never*
>> *finally fruitless.*

You are indeed the one to whom we look at all times and in all
circumstances, for you are the one who was, who is, and who is to
come. Amen.

DAY 19

Bartimaeus (2)
Mark 10:46-52

Another aspect of disciple-making is our *taking heart*. Someone who hears Bartimaeus' repeated plea turns to him and says, "Take heart, Jesus is calling you." But this is no fluffy suggestion to cheer up. Instead, we are to take heart, be of good cheer, precisely because Jesus Christ is among us now, eager to help and heal. His presence gives substance and rigour to the exhortation to "take heart."

Everywhere in Scripture this exhortation is found in the imperative. It isn't a suggestion, a recommendation, or a bit of wishful thinking. We are *commanded* to take heart, and this only because the Master has turned toward us and is now pouring out upon us exactly what we need most. He meets us precisely at the point of our pain or distress or confusion or fright. And we do take heart, for as he speaks, his word to us becomes his deed within us.

Think of the situations where these words were spoken and welcomed. A man whose guilt has paralyzed him is told to take heart, for his sins are now forgiven and his paralysis undone. A desperate woman who wants only to touch the fringe of Jesus' prayer shawl, merely make contact with him, is told to take heart, for her simple faith has healed her. Disciples who are frustrated as they try to row into a gale and who feel they are about to founder are told to take heart, for the one who quells chaos everywhere in life is with them.

Jesus Christ certainly doesn't come waltzing onto the scene with a camera-ready smile and ooze, "Cheer up, folks, it's the happy hour." Rather, just as his nearness to us first elicited from us our persistent cry for help, so his nearness has rendered effective and believable the word that makes and sustains disciples, "Take heart."

Prayer

The Psalmist has written:
> *"The Lord is my light and my salvation;*
> *whom shall I fear?*
> *The Lord is the stronghold of my life;*
> *of whom shall I be afraid?"*

Gracious God, we acknowledge our oneness with this writer as we look to you who are our light, our protection, our salvation, and as we come to you, who alone can ultimately dispel our fear.

So come upon us, we ask, in the power of your Spirit, that we shall hear our Lord's "Fear not," and hearing it, find it has taken root in us and is even now bearing fruit through us for the praise of your glory.

We thank you for him whose command to "take heart" meets with joy in us, for
> *this word we need to hear,*
> *this word he renders alive in us, and*
> *this word, his command to us and claim upon us, isn't*
> > *burdensome at all.*

We praise you for our Lord incarnate,
> *that he has lived and triumphed in the situations we*
> > *can't avoid,*
> *that his word of comfort is the word of someone afflicted*
> > *like us,*
> *that he can help us just because he has overcome what*
> > *threatens to overcome us.*

We rejoice in your grace which is
> *as many-splendoured as our needs are diverse,*
> *as far-reaching as our sin,*

as magnificent as you, the giver of grace, are yourself.

Knowing that you have commanded us to bring our requests
before you, we lift up before you for your blessing
   those who are physically blind and find our world
         inconsiderate,
   those who are emotionally blind and cannot see how they
         hurt those dearest to them,
   those who are spiritually blind and curse the darkness
      when the light of life is thrown upon them.

Use us, we ask, to assist those whose sight has failed,
            to cherish those who are insensitive,
            to pray for those whom the light has not yet
                  enlightened.
It is you, God beyond us,
      God among us,
      God within us,
whom we worship morning and evening, for you are the one
beside whom there is no other. Amen.

DAY 20

BARTIMAEUS (3)
Mark 10:46-52

Upon receiving his sight Bartimaeus immediately followed Jesus on the way, Mark informs us. There is simply no substitute for following. Mark is fond of alluding to the Christian venture as a road or way or journey. It's on the way that disciples have their understanding of God filled out and fortified. It's on the way that they learn what it is to stumble, get up again, and follow after him who is a little distance ahead of them. (He's always far enough ahead to be a leader, yet close enough not to be out of sight.) It's on the journey that they learn what it is to have their profession of loyalty to the Master collide with a world which disdains the road they are walking. To follow on the way is to forsake apathy and armchair and *live* whatever understanding of Jesus Christ we have, in whatever situation we are immersed.

While there's no substitute for following, there are many evasions. One evasion is tossing around religious clichés, stock expressions, or "code" words such as "blood" and "lamb", "process" and "liberation." Another evasion is reducing the offer and claim of the living Christ himself to a set of religious or philosophical notions that can amuse us but never move us. Another evasion is a frenzied preoccupation with committees and councils thereby confusing discipleship with water-spider activism.

Discipleship, at bottom, is always a matter of stepping out on the road and following on the way in whatever light we have received, whether great or little. If we've received illumination for one step only, let's be sure to take that step. Of course we all want such a lightning-flash as to light up our future ten years' hence. But if we knew this far in advance how our lives were going to unfold we'd either stampede after it or find ourselves paralyzed by it. Since no one can take more than one step at a time, light for just one step is always light enough. Our need, then, isn't for greater light but for greater resolve to follow him who will never fail to illuminate the step we must take. There is simply no substitute for following.

Prayer

Gracious God,
> *you have called us into the company of your Son;*
> *you have promised to nurture us with your word and*
> > *Spirit;*
> *you have promised never to fail us or forsake us.*

We know that you keep the promises you make. Today we praise you that you have shown you can be trusted and loved and adored. Then move us to do this, we pray, for with the prophet we must cry, "I have seen the Lord, sitting upon a throne, high and lifted up; and his glory fills the temple."

Because we trust your mercy we dare to make our confession to you: our look has demeaned someone;
> *our tongue has lashed someone;*
> *our gesture has dismissed someone;*
> *our silence has humiliated someone.*

Lift us up, we ask, and set our feet more firmly on the way, that we might stick closer to him who will not let our stumbling disqualify us on our journey with him.

Because we trust your care for us, we dare to make our petitions known to you; grant us
> *wisdom where we are prone to be foolish,*
> *courage where we are prone to surrender truth to*
> > *popularity;*
> *honesty where we are prone to deceive and profit from it;*

persistence where we are prone to lose patience;
cheerfulness where our negativity is prone to depress.

Stiffen our resolve, we ask, that we might stick closer to him who
plants us in the world as he was in the world.

Because we trust your compassion for all your creatures, we dare
to hold them up before you.
We plead your help
   for those whose disappointments have stalled them on the way:
      give them grace to continue;
   for those whose spill has left them wallowing on the way: give
      them grace to get up again;
   for those whose obedience has left them misunderstood by
      fellow-travellers: give them grace to know that you
      are their reward;
   for those whose faithfulness has exhilarated them on the way:
      give them grace to resist their spiritual pride.

We conclude our prayers thanking you for him who is the way,
for in him our meandering is ended,
      our pilgrimage is our joy, and
      our arrival at our destination is guaranteed. Amen.

DAY 21

The Cross (1)
John 19:17-30

What's *good* about Good Friday? Hint: mediaeval Christians spoke of the day as *God's* Friday. Good Friday was first called "God's Friday," for on this day God did something of cosmic significance. In fact, apart from what God did on this day our situation before him would have remained helpless and hopeless.

Helpless and hopeless? Yes. Jesus won't permit us to think anything else. In the all-time favourite parable the prodigal's father cries, "My son was lost; he was dead." The words *lost* and *dead* accurately describe the situation of sinful humankind before God. And then we see the brief expression by which Jesus introduces a teaching to his disciples: "If you , evil as you are...." We should note he's talking to *disciples*, not to atheists or moral degenerates or ne'er-do-wells. His assumption is so matter-of-fact: "you who are evil." And then we remember that the unrestrained joy of Christmas pertains to one thing: we've been given a Saviour. The mood of the apostles is, "Whew. At last. Just when we thought it was hopeless." And finally Jesus says without apology or argument, "I came to give myself a ransom for many [i.e., for all];I came in order to call sinners to repentance." Our Lord's diagnosis of the human situation is unmistakable.

We mustn't trivialize this diagnosis by meeting it with superficial treatment, akin to the treatment given me when I fractured my skull. I had been injured playing football on the street when I was eleven years old. I was sick, disoriented and in pain. A fellow who wanted only to be helpful put a squirt of Ozonol on my head. Obviously he didn't perceive how seriously I was injured. Or else he couldn't bring himself to face it. Perhaps he was rattled and comforted himself by saying, "Let's pretend the boy is all right." In any case, Ozonol wasn't going to do anything for a fractured skull.

Today the superficial diagnoses of the human situation are met with treatments equally superficial: moralistic self-help, self-induced religious "trips," cultural sophistication, panaceas sober and silly. Jesus Christ is infinitely more profound when he tells us we are disdainful people who have rebelled against God and are fixed in our estrangement by his just judgement.

Prayer

God eternal, the Psalmist has said that your mercy endures forever. We praise you that we can look to you wherever we are and whatever our lot, and know that the final word you speak to us will be the cross's word of mercy. Then turn our hearts and minds to you this day that we might see you, the holy one of Israel, and know that mercy welcomes us, receives us, and holds us fast.

O God, we are sobered to admit that the provision of so costly a mercy points to a need that is desperate. Your pardon is the mirror into which we peer and find ourselves startled at what stares back at us. With our mediaeval ancestors in the faith we confess, with shame, the sin whose deadliness we cannot dismiss:
> *Pride—our defiance of you and your way;*
> *Envy—our resentment that someone has appeared better than we;.*
> *Sloth—our self-pampering withdrawal from life's challenges and commitments;*
> *Avarice—our greedy insistence that we are what we possess;*
> *Gluttony—our assumption that the world's resources belong to us for the sake of our comfort;*
> *Lust—our desire to abuse your good gifts and exploit others through it;*
> *Anger—our smouldering rage, fuelling our revenge;*

And any sin whose deadliness endangers us as much as it shames us.

Give us grace to hear and believe our Lord when he describes our condition as lost and dead.
Give us grace to hear only this physician whose diagnosis, though not easy to bear, alone can help.
Give us grace to put ourselves, without reserve and without condition, into the hands of this healer that he might further his good work in us.

Today we pray for those who have not yet come to faith, who see nothing disordered about themselves which you alone can set right. Free them to see
    that their unbelief is the mark of an ungrateful rebel,
    that their inertia points to a hardened heart,
    that your judgement is as just as it is inescapable.

And then magnify your mercy before their eyes that they might embrace him whose love knows neither measure nor end. And grant that we who have gulped this mercy may so speak and live and act as to commend our Saviour to them.

It is to you, great God, that we look for our salvation, for it is you who raise the dead,
    relieve the oppressed, and
    rejoice in the restoration of your people. Amen.

DAY 22

THE CROSS (2)
John 19:17-30

Yet God's Friday is also *Good* Friday. Then it must involve good news. The good news is this: God loves us; God longs to bridge the gulf his judgement has made between us, longs to find the lost and resurrect the dead. Were God only the just judge, his rightful condemnation would be the last chapter in our story. But because God is also the loving parent, the storybook of our life remains open.

Then if God longs in love to set us right with himself, why doesn't he just go ahead and do it? Who needs the complication of a cross? But then we should think of the last time we had to discipline our children. We had to do two things. First, we had to convince our children that their behaviour was unacceptable, that we were not going to tolerate it and that their punishment was entirely deserved. Second, we had to assure our children that we still loved them, that their ill behaviour grieved us more than it grieved them, and that the punishment they had to endure was costing us much more than it was costing them. Every parent wrestles with this dilemma. God wrestles with it too. God resolves the dilemma through the cross. The cross is God's deed and word that our defiance of him is intolerable; it's also his deed and word that his love for us is unstoppable.

In Gethsemane and on the cross Jesus undergoes a dreadful estrangement from his Father. Yet since Father and Son are one in essence, one in purpose and one in its execution, we know that the Father experiences the selfsame estrangement. As Jesus dies alienated from his Father (the just judgement on

---

human sinfulness), the Father absorbs in himself the selfsame alienation. As Jesus submits to the penalty for human defiance, the Father takes his own penalty upon himself.

A parent dismisses a disobedient child to her bedroom without supper. Some time later the parent, having passed up supper himself, goes to the child's room and sits with her, explaining why all this had to occur. Then the two of them emerge from the room together. God's Friday is indeed Good Friday. There's good news for all of us.

Prayer

God eternal, it was always your plan to give us the lamb slain from the foundation of the world, for your heart has always been a heart whose love our sin could not deflect. We thank you today that the love you press upon us now is the love which greeted us at our birth and which will enfold us as we die. Then may our gratitude rise to you as often as we are moved at your care for us.

As we ponder your way with us, we chafe at the discipline you impose upon us—until we see, with the apostle, that godly discipline, however unpleasant, is grounded in your love and is needed for our growth as the people who adorn your name. Then give us grace to see your hand in our encounters with those who correct us, that you might advance us in holiness of life:
    the friend who tells us our speech is edged with sarcasm;
    the defenceless person whose hurt look confirms our
        contempt;
    the youngster who doesn't believe our evasions;
    the spouse who merely smiles when we insist we are right;
    the woman whose boldness exposes our will to power;
    the impoverished person whose stifled child questions
        our privilege and affluence.

Just as you used the prophet Nathan to confront the king with the darker recesses of his own heart, so we ask you to keep on using the people whose lives intersect ours, for we plead for release from

the deformities of spirit which warp us and wound others.
As we ponder your way with us, give us grace to know
that you love us with a love that never lets us off and a
love that never lets us go;
that your judgement upon us is the first step in your
restoration of us;
that our identity as Christ's is the truth about us now and
the truth about us eternally.

And as we hear you speak your word of judgement and grace,
let us drop our defences;
let us submit to you;
let us welcome whatever is needed that we might be sons
and daughters of the light.

We praise you
for parents whose love and patience and firmness reflected
yours,
for schoolteachers who were entrusted with us,
for youth leaders who shaped us as they learned of you,
for friends in Christ whose honesty with us spared us grief.

As we ponder your way with us, we bow before the suffering of
our Lord, whose estrangement from you was more than we can
grasp,
whose faithfulness to you we extol, and by
whose sacrifice we are saved.

O merciful God, we praise you, we adore you, we commit
ourselves to you afresh; for you have embraced us all in the arms
of the crucified. Amen

DAY 23

THE CROSS (3)
John 19:17-30

The "good news" of the cross quickens a response in us. There are several aspects to it. It includes our acknowledgement that the cure has been fashioned by God and pressed into our hands. It includes our admission that we neither add to this cure nor subtract from it: either we receive it or we walk away from it. It includes our awareness that the cure, finally, is not an "it" but the living, loving person of our Lord, and therefore we are to embrace him in believing, trusting gratitude.

One hundred and fifty years ago it was the custom for the leaders of a vanquished army to hand over their swords to the victor. Handing over one's sword was the conclusive, public acknowledgement of surrender. After the Duke of Wellington had triumphed in the battle of Waterloo he summoned the defeated French generals to his tent. They came, greeting Wellington and congratulating him on his superior military prowess. They were professional soldiers too and they had an eye for military genius. In fact they admitted that because Wellington was so fine a soldier it was no insult to lose to him. It was an honour just to be found on the field of battle with him. Perhaps they should have a glass of sherry and toast him. The flattery mounted. Wellington listened to it for twenty minutes. Then he said very quietly, yet very emphatically, "Gentlemen, I want your swords." He didn't want to be flattered; he wanted them to surrender. And he wanted a conclusive, public acknowledgement of that surrender. They were going to have to stand before him empty-handed. It is for the same reason that the hymnwriter cries, "*Nothing* in my hand I bring; simply to thy cross I cling."

Prayer

*God eternal, there rings in our ears the refrain which we, your
people, shall never forget: "I shall be your God and you shall be
my people." We praise you that you have promised to stand by us
and stand for us in all the tides and turbulence of life. We thank
you that you have constrained us to respond to you. We ask you
now to purify our discipleship that our single-minded
determination to be your people might permeate all that we do,
all that we say, all that we hope to be.*

*We intercede today for those whose hearing of the word of the
cross is blunted by their difficulties:*
    the single parent who feels utterly abandoned;
    *the unmarried person who finds a couple-oriented society
        inconsiderate;*
    the adolescent whose insecurities seem not to be understood;
    *the unemployed worker whose self-esteem has been
        shattered;*
    the homemaker whose daily routine is dreary and dull;
    *the nursing-home resident who frets over being a burden
        and a nuisance;*
    *the business people who are pressed and pressured until
        they can think of nothing besides finances.*

*In all these situations, O God, we plead the penetration of your
Spirit, for only then shall the cares of this life abate enough*
    to let us hear your word;
    to reorder our priorities;
    *to simplify our lives as we seek first your kingdom and
        your righteousness.*

*We pray as well for ourselves as those who have responded to the
word of the cross. Help us to see that*
    the surrender we made we must make again and again;
    *the love we declared in a moment of enthusiasm we must
        declare when we are discouraged;*

*the loyalty we announced when Christ our King appeared
    to us in his splendour we must uphold when he
    comes to us in the poor, the wretched, the repulsive;
the obedience we clung to when we were floundering we must
    honour when our self-confidence knows no bounds.*

*It is to you, O God, that we look at all times and in all
circumstances; for it is you alone who have
    created us,
    reconciled us,
    called us and
    commissioned us to a life of service.
May your name be praised. Amen.*

DAY 24

THE HOLY SPIRIT:
GOD'S POWER IN MISSION (1)
Acts 1:6-8

In both the Hebrew and Greek languages the word translated "spirit" also means "wind." By extension it signifies that movement of air or wind which is breath. For primitive people breath is the life-principle, the vital sign. Where there is breath there is life.

Jesus Christ is the bearer and the bestower of God's Spirit. He is charged with the vitality of God in order to impart it. The Spirit, then, is God lending life to what otherwise remains dead.

In the New Testament the Spirit is linked pre-eminently to mission. Each written gospel, detailing the life and work of the one who himself was sent from the Father, ends on a mission theme. It's as though the ministry, death and resurrection of Jesus have primed his followers for mission. They need only empowering. The gospels conclude by pointing to that empowering. When the Spirit is added, the Christian mission explodes.

Let's be sure of this: the power which Jesus supplies for his mission is the only power which accomplishes his work. Where his power is not prayed for and relied on, where people think that they can render mission effective and engineer results, a grave distortion develops. Coercion is used. At one time the coercion was physical (the Crusades.) Centuries later the coercion was social: if you weren't affiliated with the church you were denied business and political opportunity, even citizenship and human rights. Most recently the coercion has been psychological: "Faith in God will make you wealthy, popular, a winner."

The truth is, since power is the capacity to achieve purpose, only God can supply the vitality that renders his own mission effective. Concerning this mission we are called to be faithful. This is *our* responsibility. Success is *God's* responsibility, and God's alone. We ought not to try to exchange responsibilities with him. It's enough that our faithfulness, birthed and sustained by God's promise, ever be found trusting his promise. For God has promised that the one who was raised from the dead; this one who uniquely bears the Spirit will bestow the selfsame Spirit freely and fully to invigorate his own mission. And the promises God makes he always keeps. God's breath assuredly lends life to the witness of his people and to all who receive that witness.

Prayer

Gracious God,
> *you do not need us yet you choose not to be without us;*
> *you are the holy one of Israel yet you endure the sin of the*
> > *world;*
> *you are the author of life yet you have tasted our death;*
> *you are high and lifted up yet you indwell the humblest of*
> > *your people.*

We praise you that you are richer than we can imagine, for our thoughts cannot confine you or our ways control you.
> *Breathe into us the life which you are.*
> *Speak to us the word of your love.*
> *Lift us above ease and convention.*
> *Free our hearts and mouths that we might thank you*
> > *whose riches shall be ours forever.*

We praise you today for our Lord Jesus Christ, for his resolute insistence that he must do the work of you who sent him.
We ask that the Spirit which was in him and is now in us might
> *prove yet more fruitful in our lives.*

So it is we ask you to equip us for mission, especially
        when indifferent people question our zeal,
        when fellow disciples suspect our discernment,
        when opposition leaves us frustrated,
        when the way of the cross seems pointless.

Our Lord has said that you give your Spirit without measure. Then in your boundless generosity fill us with that selfsame Spirit, for we want to be your agents and ambassadors in your world.

We repent of the stain we placed on your name when we
        disdained you.
We repent of the harm we have done in imposing our schedules
        and our plans on you.
We repent of slandering our Lord
        as we Christians abused "the apple of his eye", the Jews,
        as we sowed the seeds of apartheid,
        as we exploited the native peoples of this land,
        as we curried favour with the rich and powerful,
        as we neglected the resourceless, the defenceless, and the
                voiceless.

Accept our penitence, we plead. Suffuse us with your pardon. Illuminate us anew that we might never confuse our schemes for success with your vocation to servanthood.

In all of this, remind us again that we are sent by him
        who had nowhere to lay his head,
        who urged us to count the cost,
        who yet promised us his help, and
        whose hold on his people never loosens.

You are the God on whom we can rely. For this we praise you and thank you and honour you. Amen.

DAY 25

THE HOLY SPIRIT: GOD'S POWER IN MISSION (2)
1 Corinthians 12:4-7

As the Spirit-empowered mission invigorates us we are gathered into the church, a fellowship of the Holy Spirit. The Spirit is the bond-fast glue that binds diverse individuals into an authentic community.

"I doubt it," the cynic objects, "the Spirit has nothing to do with it. Why not admit that what holds church members together is social class, economic equality, educational uniformity, or racial uniqueness?" Is the cynic correct—and therefore no cynic at all? Is the bond of our fellowship not the Spirit but something that the sociologist can measure? In the church at Antioch we see Barnabas, formerly a rich landowner from Cyprus; Symeon, a black Gentile; Lucius, a Jew from North Africa; Paul a Jew who has committed himself to the company of Gentiles. Paul himself disliked intensely some of the theology which came out of the Jerusalem church. Nevertheless, he visited that congregation regularly and organized a relief fund when those people were starving. Only the Spirit could hold such diverse people together. The bond of our fellowship is the breath which God breathes into his community when the congregation welcomes someone who left school in grade five and can't speak grammatical English; when the welfare recipient is received gladly; when the woman on Social Assistance takes a taxi home from the supermarket the day she receives her cheque (because it's the one day she can hold her head up) and nobody faults her for it; when the bank executive is loved the day after his bank has shut down the biggest employer in town; when hospitality is given the new black family, whose father is white.

In Corinth, as in any congregation, the supply of gifts and talents was matched by the reservoir of jealousy, bitterness and strife. For this reason Paul insisted that the Spirit bound Christians to one another only as the Spirit engendered love among them. Such love, he insisted, "doesn't pursue selfish advantages, isn't touchy, doesn't keep account of evil, can outlast anything. *It is the one thing that still stands when all else has fallen.*" Such love, fostered by so great a Spirit, will ever breathe life into any collection or crowd, transforming all such self-protecting persons into the community of God's people.

Prayer

Gracious God, you have always wanted a people for yourself. We praise you that you have called and preserved and equipped that people which you summon to stand with you as you stand with them. We rejoice in your wisdom, your goodness, your patience and your purpose. Move us ever to glorify, obey, and thank you who do all things well.

We thank you for believers in the different Christian families who are your children:
> *Eastern Orthodox with their love of tradition;*
> *Anglicans whose liturgies will enrich us forever;*
> *Baptists who know that we must do our own believing;*
> *Presbyterians who point us to the sovereignty of God;*
> *Methodists who urge us to holiness of life;*
> *Pentecostals whose joy in the Spirit lifts us;*
> *Quakers whose silent waiting on you deepens us.*

Let us learn from our sisters and brothers and cherish their contribution even as we share ours with them. Save us from that family feud which dishonours our Lord and impedes his work. For he has sheep not of our fold.

Just as your Spirit enlarged Peter's mind and heart, moving him to receive those he had previously scorned, so we pray your Spirit

*to do as much for us, that our congregation might welcome all
whom our Saviour has redeemed:*

> *the ex-convict whom we suspect;*
> *the welfare recipient whose spending pattern we criticize;*
> *the juvenile vandal whose upbringing we deplore;*
> *the chronically deranged whom we fear;*
> *the embittered who can't see why any of these people
> should be supported.*

*Save us from restricting our welcome to those who are like us,
who do not annoy us, and who never contradict us. For our Lord
has sheep not of our fold.*

*As love is the principal fruit of your Spirit, O God, and the basis
of all other fruits, we pray for an increase of love within us.
Magnify in us a love which is patient and kind, not boastful or
irritable or resentful, bearing and enduring and hoping all things.*

*As great as our need is, we acknowledge your grace to be greater
still. We praise you that this grace will ever support, correct, and
inflame us. Amen.*

DAY 26

THE HOLY SPIRIT: GOD'S POWER IN MISSION (3)

Romans 8:9-11

Who, ultimately is drawn into the community whose bond is the Spirit? Who is the beneficiary of the Christian mission? It's the individual. For while God may deal with a people, he speaks only to individuals (as the Hebrew Bible makes clear.) Jesus himself insists that he leave the ninety-nine sheep and go looking for one.

Now once a shepherd has found the sheep, getting it home is easy. He picks it up (if it is small) or drives it (if it is big.) But human beings aren't handled in this manner. We are endowed with a God-ordained human integrity that God doesn't violate. He doesn't compel or coerce. The characteristic effectiveness of the Spirit's moving within us is this: the Spirit convinces without coercing, persuades without pulverizing, wins without wrenching. The Spirit is the power by which Jesus Christ convinces people of his reality and truth without violating them. There are two ways of having your daughter marry a Frenchman. One is to bring a fellow from France and force her to marry him. The other is to send her to France and let her fall in love with a Frenchman. The Spirit is the breath/wind/power of God bringing Jesus to us and us to him, in such a manner that we aren't forced into his company but rather are moved to receive him as he elicits our wonder and adoration, loyalty and love.

There happen to be two New Testament words for "good." One word is "good" in the sense of correct, circumspect, upright. (It's in this sense that Mark Twain has Huckleberry Finn ask God to make the bad people good and the good people nice.) The second word describes as good someone whose goodness

---

is attractive, winsome, inviting, engaging. It's in this latter sense of "good" that the gospel writer speaks of Jesus as the Good Shepherd. The Spirit is the breath he inhales himself and exhales upon us as we find in him a winsomeness, an attractiveness that melts and warms the human heart and even moves yet another individual to become a disciple and follow after him forever.

Prayer

Gracious God, Augustine has said that you love each of us as if each were the only one for you to love. We cannot comprehend the depth of your love for us, yet we know that you cherish us when we cannot cherish ourselves. As your love floods us, may it overflow onto love-parched lives which will blossom and redound to your praise.

We thank you for that gentle Spirit who has whispered to us, nudged us, and pointed us to your truth.
We admit our enduring need of correction,
for we are prone to wander;
our enduring need of forgiveness,
for we are prone to sin;
our enduring need of guidance,
for we are prone to stumble;
our enduring need of conviction,
for we are prone to evade your truth.

O send your Spirit upon us again and again, we ask, for his warmth and light and refreshing shower will increase the harvest of our righteousness.

We ask you to refine us in the fire of the Spirit, for then our lives will shine forth as gold whose impurities have been removed. At whatever cost, through whatever discomfort, burn out of us
the arrogance which sees no deep-seated depravity;
the deceit which masquerades as cleverness;

*the put-down gesture which regards another person as not
    worth hearing;
the haughty look which silences the criticism we deserve;
the glibness which trifles with another's perplexity and pain.*

*The apostle tells us that you, our God, refine your people because
you deem us precious. Then confirm us as your people as you melt
us, mould us, fill us and use us.*

*We thank you for the people whose firm but gentle way with us
has reflected your activity within us:
    the friend who set us right without embarrassing us;
    the parent whose discipline was mixed with kindness;
    the teacher whose truthful speech was softened by caring eyes;
    our Lord himself, whose yoke has proved easy and whose
        burden is light.*

*Great God, you surround us with blessings as numberless as the
sands on the shore. For this we adore you now and forever. Amen.*

DAY 27

THE HOLY SPIRIT: GOD'S POWER IN MISSION (4)

Romans 8:15; Galatians 3:2

We of the historic Protestant churches tend to be sceptical about any talk relating the Spirit to human experience. As soon as "Christian experience" is mentioned we envisage an emotional extravaganza accompanied by loss of self-control. Or we think of the religious exploiter and his disreputable sleaze. Despite our apprehension, however, the church of the apostolic era exhibits Spirit-invigorated experience everywhere. Paul comes upon some Christians in Galatia who are distorting the gospel through which they came to faith. He corrects them by reminding them of their experience: "Did you receive the Spirit by works of the law or by hearing with faith? Did you experience so many things in vain?" His question points them back to an identifiable occurrence. It's as though he said, "Did you get your headache last week by drinking too much coffee or by colliding with a door-frame?"

While the life-experience which confirms the presence and power of the Spirit is rich and varied, we should probe an aspect of it which is bedrock for the New Testament church. For these people had had drawn out of them, from the deepest depths of their hearts, the exclamation, "Abba, Father." (Romans 8:15) "Abba" was the term a Palestinian youth used to speak of his father. Reverent Jews never used it of God lest they appear presumptuous. Early-day Christians uttered it because they couldn't help uttering it: the Spirit had torn it from them. Just as the person in pain can't help groaning, and the person tickled by a good joke can't help laughing, so the person whom the Spirit has penetrated can't help crying out, "Father, my father." For such a person has overwhelming confirmation of her adoption as God's child.

Paul refers to a similar experience of the Spirit in terms of a pledge or down payment. Our experience of our Lord's kindness, pardon, encouragement, and companionship is a down payment: what we have received is a pledge that more is coming. The Greek word the apostle uses is found in modern Greek, where it denotes a woman's engagement ring. Delighted and enriched as she is now in her most intimate relationship, the ring is yet a promise of more and better to come.

Prayer

Gracious God, we approach you today only because you first approached us.

> *You have opened our eyes to your nearness.*
> *You have unstopped our ears to your word.*
> *You have thawed our hearts by your kindness.*
> *You have quickened our love by yours.*

We thank you today for the apostle Paul, whose intimacy with your Spirit has inspired countless Christians.
We praise you for

> *his steadfastness in the face of detractors,*
> *his forgiveness in the face of slander,*
> *his courage in the face of setbacks,*
> *his faithfulness in the face of harassment.*

Grant that the apostle whose life meant Christ and whose death could only mean more of his Lord might ever prod us, challenge us, correct us and hold up before us the one whom he knew and will enjoy forever.

Just as the cry, "Abba, Father", was torn out of ancient Christians as your Spirit surged over them, grant that the same cry might be torn out of us, for your Spirit has made us your children as well.
Then save us from thinking ourselves orphaned

> *when the storms of life chill us,*
> *when doubt gnaws at us,*

when fear seeps into us,
when temptation unsettles us.

So expand the work of your Spirit in our hearts that we shall ever know ourselves to be Abba's, nourished at his table, and delighting in his family.

We remember with gratitude John Wesley whose "heart was strangely warmed" by your Spirit and whose flame of faith warmed, illuminated and cheered thousands as it kindled a fire in them as well. Bind us to all whose experience of you is real and rich, for then we shall speed each other on the way as we await what you have in store for us.

It is you, O God, whose Spirit assures us of riches beyond what we can ask or think. And it is you, O God, whose richness will ever elicit our praise. Amen.

DAY 28

THE CHURCH (1)
Romans 10:14-15.

The church is where we hear and ponder all that we have discussed so far. It's where we find ourselves inflamed to do the truth in God's world, where we are encouraged and helped by fellow seekers, strugglers and witnesses. Yet there are markedly different understandings of the church. Let's look at three traditional ways of understanding the church.

Many Christians maintain that the church consists of those who gather to hear the word of God preached. Not surprisingly, in most of the church buildings of this tradition the pulpit stands square in the centre, elevated; it can't be overlooked. People assemble to be taught something. The clergy are identified in terms of the most important thing they do: preach.

Christians who think along this line emphatically believe that Christian truth has a precise content. God is ultimately the author of this content. Preachers are God's spokespersons, and no one can afford to be uninformed or misinformed with respect to God's truth. The church consists of those who gather to be informed. What's more, the other side of this conviction is the insistence that we can't inform ourselves of the gospel by means of movies or magazines, bird watching, water-skiing or line-dancing.

Frequently we are told that we don't have to gather regularly to learn of the will and work of God. We can learn it all from nature: sunrise, ocean waves, thunderstorms. But what is learned of *God* from nature? Will the ocean wave ever tell us how ingrained our sinfulness is? Will a squirrel eating nuts steep us in God's forgiveness? And will the hurricane quicken us to respond in adoration, love and obedience to the God who has been to hell and back for us? Will a flower's scent call us to live for social justice?

Then historic Protestants evidently have a point: proclamation must inform us of who God is for us and who we are to be for him. Jesus began his public ministry by preaching. He called others to do as much. This understanding of the church can't be set aside lightly.

Prayer

The Psalmist has written, "He put a new song in my mouth, a song of praise to our God". Gracious God, we approach you today with joy, knowing that it is your new song, pressed upon us, which has warmed our heart and opened our mouth,
quickened our praise and lifted it to you.

Today we praise you especially for those people who have helped us to hear your gospel, to believe its truth, and to obey its claim. So it is we remember before you, with thanksgiving,
the parent who schooled us in Scripture when we were very
young,
the Sunday school teacher whose faith fostered ours even
when we didn't know it,
the minister whose zeal for your kingdom loomed larger
than his personal idiosyncracies,,
the friend who explained yet again the gospel truth we had
forgotten,
the simple Christian whose intimacy with her Lord spoke
more tellingly than anything she said,
the author we never met, yet whose books rendered him a
beacon in a dark night and a comfort in our distress.
For all these people we thank you at this time, knowing it is through them you gave us so much which now moves us to sing, to shout, to exult in the name of you, our God.

We know that you have yet more light and truth to bring forth from your Holy Word. Then come upon us afresh that we might

hear our Lord Jesus Christ in the words of
> *Moses, whose law will shape the lives of your people*
> > *forever,*
> *Elijah, who urges us to listen for you in the still, small*
> > *voice,*
> *David, who assures us that you will use us in spite of our*
> > *sin,*
> *Amos, whose outrage at injustice and oppression must*
> > *awaken the same in us,*
> *Hosea, who knows that you will not, cannot, give up*
> *on your people.*

We pray you to give us
> *the spirit of Deborah, who recognized your victory over*
> > *your enemies,*
> *the spirit of Mary, who waited for greater understanding*
> > *of your will and way,*
> *the spirit of Magdalene, who found herself wholly*
> > *cleansed by her Lord,*
> *the spirit of an unnamed woman in Rome who was a*
> > *mother to Paul.*
We ask this because we crave a deeper work of grace in us, and
thank you that you have promised to grant it to us.

We pray for greater grasp of your word written, that through it
we might
> *distinguish your truth from the falsehoods which whisper*
> > *to us,*
> *see where it challenges our compliance with principalities*
> > *and powers,*
> *love your world with a love as widespread as the arms of*
> > *him to whom all Scripture points, the crucified*
> > *himself.*

For it is the fear of you, our God, which shall ever be the
beginning and continuation of our wisdom. Amen.

DAY 29

THE CHURCH (2)
Romans 12:4-5

There is yet another understanding of the church which is cherished by many Christians. These Christians emphasize the church as the body of Christ. Paul certainly speaks of the body and of Jesus himself as the head of that body. As soon as this truth sinks into us we are jolted: it's clear that we are related to Jesus Christ only insofar as we are related to the church, his body. (After all, in everyday life we relate to whole persons, never to severed heads.) We have no identity as Christians once we are detached from the body. The apostle himself asks, "Of what use is a detached leg?" No use at all, obviously. Furthermore, is it really a leg? If a leg is that which supports and propels a torso, then a detached leg is no leg at all. It's merely a clump of tissue, of no apparent use to anyone or anything. Christians in the church-as-body tradition remind us that we can be Christian (and can be used as Christians) only as long as we are related to the whole of Jesus Christ, body as well as head.

"But surely 'body of Christ' doesn't refer to the local congregation unless it's qualified a thousand times over," someone remarks, "because the local congregation is riddled with bickering, power-plays and in-fighting." But in fact the local congregation *is* our Lord's body. His body may be scarred, marred, pockmarked, even deformed. Nevertheless, it's the only body he has. And it's this body, whether graceful or grotesque, which he must use and will use to do his work among men, women and children.

A glorious aspect of this Roman Catholic/Anglican emphasis is this: the body will evidently last as long as the head lasts. And since the head will last, the church will certainly endure.

The powers of death can't prevail against it. Our panic is defused, then, and our patience prolonged.

Is the church weak? God will strengthen it. Confused? God will enlighten it. Corrupt? God will purify it. The body of the risen, triumphant Christ will endure for as long as he himself endures. Of course we mustn't trade on this, sparing ourselves care and concern, zeal and sacrifice. But we *are* spared anxiety, impatience and, above all, despair.

Prayer

The Psalmist has written,
> *"God is our refuge and strength,*
> > *a very present help in trouble,*
> *therefore we will not fear."*

Gracious God, we bow before you today for we know that you are finally our only refuge and strength, even as we know you are a sufficient refuge and strength. It is you who fulfill in us the command of our Lord, "Fear not." Then it is to you that we now look and lift up our hearts in praise and adoration, for it is you who have stayed our fear and strengthened our weak knees as your refuge became that peace which the world neither gives nor takes away. We thank you that you are the same for us as you were to our foreparents and will be to our children.

We lift up for your blessing those of our congregation who together are the body of Christ, even as we thank you for their particular gifts:
> *the elderly woman whose radiance outstrips the tragedy she has known;*
> *the youngest child whose wide-eyed wonder dissolves our jadedness;*
> *the perceptive thinker who speaks for those whose gift is not speech,*
> *the intellectually challenged adult whose guileless affection enlivens ours;*

the firebrand who keeps before us that suffering which the
church's head has not forgotten;
the singers and poets who express the depth and passion
of our response to you.

Wherever the church, the body of Christ, has become flabby from
self-indulgence, correct it;
Wherever it has become slovenly through indifference, renew its
zeal;
Wherever it has been lulled asleep, startle it;
Wherever it has come to tolerate what its Lord abhors, awaken it;
Wherever it has become callous for any reason at all, show it the
wounds of the crucified, wounds which the world
must ever see in it.

O King eternal, the apostle insists that the body is knit together
in love. Then magnify among your people
that love which will indeed knit up whatever has become
unravelled,
that love which has renounced the ambition of "me first,"
that love which rejoices at no wrong but is delighted with
the right,
that love without which the gifts of the members promote
only envy.
Increase such love in us until we glow with the love of him who
gave himself for others in self-forgetfulness, and who now calls us
to do the same.

As we gaze upon him we see you, our God, whose mercy and
faithfulness will call forth our gratitude in life, in death, and in
life beyond death. Amen.

DAY 30

THE CHURCH (3)

Romans 8:9-11; 1 Corinthians 6:9-11

The emphasis of some other Christians is different again. They insist that the church is characterized by the Spirit. In fact the church is the community of the Spirit. These people remind us that a body can appear resplendent and yet be a corpse. It's the Spirit alone who renders the body living.

Now to emphasize the Spirit is to direct attention to our acquaintance with God. Early-day believers weren't at all reluctant to speak of it. The letter to the Hebrews tells us of those who have "tasted the goodness of the word of God and the powers of the age to come." These disciples hadn't merely read about the richness of God and discussed it endlessly; they had intimate acquaintance with the living reality of God. The Spirit was God himself surging over his people, pressing himself upon them, stamping them with his imprint, identifying them ("you are mine") forever.

We must never underestimate the difference which the infusion of the Spirit makes. Without the Spirit we merely "say prayers;" with the Spirit we pray. Without the Spirit we move mechanically through religious exercises; with the Spirit we worship. Without the Spirit a congregation knows only middle-class manners; with the Spirit it is bathed in love. Without the Spirit there is a weekly religious address; with the Spirit there is a witness manifestly inflamed and empowered. A church where Christian experience isn't suspected but welcomed; a church where the Spirit's certainty is sought and celebrated, where the truth which the mind grasps is ignited and is seen to transform life; such a church is surely the "spiritual house" of which Peter speaks, constructed from those living stones who have themselves been sculpted from *the* living stone.

It can't be denied that the Spirit characterizes early Christian awareness. The newer churches of our era have done much to remind the church universal of the necessary balance between mind and heart, light and warmth.

All three emphases are needed. And for the rich testimony of all three traditions God is to be praised. For as Jesus says, our Father knows what we need even before we ask him.

Prayer

The prophet has written, "Not by might, nor by power, but by my Spirit, says the Lord of hosts."

We praise you, O God, that it is not by coercion or tyranny but by your Spirit that you make us and mould us. For
> *your Spirit is the rain which makes the parched earth fruitful;*
> *your Spirit is the breeze which refreshes the tired traveller;*
> *your Spirit is the fire which warms the chilled heart;*
> *your Spirit is the patient love which calls us away from our self-protection and beckons us to abandon ourselves to you.*

We thank you that this is who you are, for to this God our hearts go out and our spirits rise and our praise ascends. Hear us today as we pour out our burdens and our needs, our intercessions and our thanksgivings.

We thank you for your people who have known you not as idea or sentiment but as the living, sovereign God, whose ways are not our ways yet whose compassion constrains you to dwell among your people, sharing our pain, shouldering our shame, lifting us to you that you might fit us to your purpose.
Among such people we remember before you
> *Mother Teresa, who saw her Lord in the face of the*

dying and destitute,
William Booth, who met you in an urban slum,
Dietrich Bonhoeffer, whose faithfulness to you meant his
death,
Martin Luther King, who knew that the clenched fist and
the smoking gun do not advance your kingdom.
We praise you that their difficulties did not obscure their joy nor their afflictions their contentment. We thank you that by your Spirit you called them, equipped them, moved them to content themselves in you. We rejoice in the coming day when the church militant becomes the church triumphant and we, with them, shall see our Lord face-to-face.

Grant that your Spirit might ever brood over us,
lifting out of us the heart-cry we cannot articulate,
empowering the praise too deep for words,
igniting the truth which has long lain inert,
binding into one family the diverse people whom you
have called as witnesses and workers.

Grant us now a more ardent love for your church in all its diversity, for just as your people are as numberless as the stars in the heavens, so are we as varied as snowflakes, and so rich is the body of him in whom are hid all the treasures of wisdom and knowledge.

For him, and for that Spirit which he pours upon us his people, we praise you and honour you for ever and ever. Amen.

DAY 31

SIN (1)

Genesis 3:1-7; 22-24; Luke 13:34.

The church is said to exist for sinners. Is the word "sin" as obsolete as a horseless carriage, chugging along in an antique car parade? Many would say, "Yes. The term has outlived its usefulness. Find another." Yet when Paul Tillich, an untraditional philosopher and theologian, was interviewed by *Time* magazine, he said, "For twenty-five years I have tried to find another word. There is no other word." Karl Menninger, internationally known psychiatrist and founder of the Menninger Clinic, has written a bestseller, *Whatever Became of Sin?* It appears that we can't dismiss the word.

Then let's be sure we know what the word means. Sin is telling God to "buzz off." The telling may be explicit and fully conscious. But more often it's implicit and disguised. In any case the bottom line is the same. God is told to get lost. When the ever-generous one lavishes upon us what we need most, we resent the interference. When the same one calls and claims us, we say, "Hands off." The root sin (and the source of all concrete sins) is an arrogant posture of defiance, rejection and repudiation. It might appear that we have innocently (because accidentally) overlooked God, but the innocence is only apparent: our hearts are riddled with contempt.

Children's stories frequently depict an aristocrat setting out on a walk. He steps around peasants and paupers, disdaining them. In his aristocratic aloofness he never really sees them, notes them, or perceives their claim upon him: for him they simply *aren't*. As the story unfolds, one of the peasants or paupers turns out to be a prince or princess. The aristocrat's proud aloofness has caused him to forfeit something of unspeakable value: intimacy with royalty. Men and women strut like aristocrats disdaining the God who, in the Son, is lowly and humble. God's self-renouncing condescension we regard as weakness. The God whose coming among us is so ordinary as to be dismissible we proceed to dismiss. When, in Christ, he does plant himself in front of us and presses both his mercy and his claim upon us we thoughtlessly wave him aside.

Sin is our defiance, rejection and repudiation of the living God.

Prayer

The prophet Micah writes:
> *"Who is a God like unto thee, pardoning iniquity and*
> *passing over transgression...?*
> *Thou wilt cast all our sins into the depths of the sea."*

Eternal God, it is with hearts made glad by your mercy that we approach you today, for your mercy confronts us with our sin only to bear it away as well. We rejoice in the steadfast love
> *which you are eternally,*
> *which you have made concrete in Jesus Christ, and*
> *which your Spirit now pours upon us from moment to*
> *moment.*

Hear us as we search our hearts. For we do so not in a mood of self-indulgent wallowing but in the confidence of those who know that the sin which is cast up before us you will not fail to cast into the depths of the sea.

We confess that we have waved you aside
> *when your truth contradicted our inflated opinion of*
> *ourselves and others,*
> *when your claim thwarted the plans we had made*
> *without thought of you,*
> *when your grace confirmed us in our weakness and need,*
> *when your pardon challenged our continuing complicity*

in sin.

We plead for greater sensitivity to you in your approach to us.
Open our eyes to the neighbour whose appearance bespeaks
his distress.
Open our ears to the neighbour whose cry tells us of her
broken heart.
Open our hearts to the neighbour whose silence suggests a
suffering too deep for words.
Open our minds to the neighbour who can lift our thinking
out of the grooves of prejudice.
Open our hands to the neighbour whom we can help and
hold and heal.
For our Lord insists that to encounter such neighbours is to
encounter you, our God.

We thank you that you are in yourself all that sinners need to
find in you:
a judge who cannot be deceived;
a parent who provides for wayward children;
a humble person who absorbs the penalty we
deserve;
a healer whose hand will ever give wholeness.

We bless you for your prophet Micah, for you moved him to write
of you, "He will again have compassion upon us." It is you whom
we worship, you whose compassion will mark you for ever. Amen.

DAY 32

SIN (2)

Romans 1:28-30; Mark 7:14-23

There are, of course, inescapable consequences of our high-handedness. The first is estrangement from God. He isn't indifferent to our postured superiority. He reacts. He thrusts us away from him. He won't allow us to denounce him, defy him, and continue to remain intimate with him at the same time. An abyss opens up between God and us. The one who is eternally Father now looks upon alienated sons and daughters. The ruler confronts rebellious subjects. Created to be God's partners, co-workers and friends, we relentlessly conspire against God; we sabotage God's work and disdain his word; we trade on God's friendship—or think we can.

The second consequence is estrangement from our sisters and brothers. When I was very young and warring with my sisters, my mother would say in exasperation, "Why can't you just get along?" Well, why couldn't we? A Samaritan woman says to Jesus, "You are a Jew. I am a Samaritan. Samaritans don't have anything to do with Jews. And that's how it is." Why is all of human existence conflict-riddled? The first question in Scripture is addressed to Adam and Eve, every man and every woman, after they have alienated themselves from God: "Where are you?" says God. The second question is addressed to Cain after he has murdered his alienated brother: "Where is your brother?" Yes. Where is my brother, my sister? An abyss has opened up between us.

If the sociologists could eliminate the social conditions that are the occasion of human conflict, there would still be no enduring utopia, for the cause of human conflict would remain untouched. The cause is that profoundest inner disorder rooted in our defiance and disobedience concerning

God.

The third consequence of God's judicial reaction to our root sin is alienation from ourselves. An abyss opens up, somehow, between me and myself. You see, God can be refused. But we were made for God and will be most authentically human only in him. To refuse God is somehow to refuse ourselves. It's no wonder we are chronically discontent, *dis*-eased, self-alienated; no wonder we keep asking, "What's wrong with me?"—when in fact everyone is suffering from the same ailment for the same reason. It's no wonder we keep anaesthetizing ourselves with playthings. Yet every so often the anaesthetic breaks down and people are startled to find that "it's still there"—the haunting apprehension that there is something of the innermost me that I'm missing but can't quite find.

Prayer

Gracious God, we praise you today that you care for us, that your care persists in the face of every affront and every frustration. Give us grace now to seek you, submit to you, and serve you, for you are the one who has made us, has saved us, and now summons us to acknowledge you before men and women everywhere. Deepen our adoration as you magnify our thankfulness and praise.

Eternal God, it is your Spirit who undoes our defensiveness, subdues our haughtiness, and crumbles our self-righteousness. So it is your Spirit who frees us to confess the estrangement which isolates us at every turn. For we are indeed alienated
from you, the friend whose love and truth we need yet
ignore,
from our spouse, the companion we are given to cherish
and embrace,
from our children, who are to find in us a model of your
care for them,
from our colleagues, whose partnership with us is afflicted

with abrasiveness,
from our profoundest self, whose absence fosters a rootless,
nameless disquiet forever seeping into us when we expect
it least.

It is for you, O God, that we are made.
It is in you, O Christ, that we are redeemed.
It is through you, O Spirit, that we must be turned back to our
God, to God's world, and to that self which awaits us all. Fulfill
our inmost longing and meet our inmost need as we know more
richly the one whose embrace enables us to embrace him in
gratitude and gladness.

Just as our Lord Jesus Christ has reconciled us to you, O God, by
absorbing the hostility of us to whom he was sent, so make us
agents of reconciliation as we absorb the hostility of those among
whom we live:
people whose racial distinctions divide them,
people whose economic disparity drives them apart,
people whose religious expressions raise fences,
people whose pain has made them bitter.
Grant unto us the grace of our Lord who has appointed us his
ambassadors and has entrusted us with the ministry of
reconciliation.

We conclude our prayer praising you for that mercy which sought
us, found us, and will enfold us for ever and ever. Amen.

DAY 33

SIN (3)

Ephesians 2:1-10

"What a downer the last few pages have been," someone complains. But not really. You see, the most optimistic thing to be said of any of us is that we are sinners.

If we aren't sinners then are we sick? But "sick" has dubious connotations today, and they aren't going to help us at all. Besides, what's the point of using "sick" when we don't have a physician with curative powers equal to the ailment? Then would it be preferable to describe humankind as socially maladjusted? To say this, however, is to invite social engineering. And the mere prospect of social engineering should frighten us, especially in view of the social experimentation of the last century. For the "engineers," the "answer" people, will insist upon the right to enforce their social solutions. They can only put us on the road to totalitarianism. The safest thing to say, because it's the truest thing to say, is also the most optimistic thing to say: we are sinners.

We must note that when we say men and women are sinners we are not using "are" in the same way as when we say that horses are four-legged. To say that a horse is four-legged is to say that it's meant to be four-legged; it's supposed to be nothing else and is never going to be anything else, since four-leggedness is essential to a horse's definition. When we say that we are sinners we say, on the contrary, that we *aren't* meant to be sinners; we aren't supposed to be such and will, by God's grace, become something else. To speak of ourselves as sick or socially maladjusted is pessimistic because it's hopeless. But to speak of ourselves as sinners is profoundly optimistic. For we can, right now, be restored by and restored to the God who makes all things new.

Jesus comes upon different people in different kinds of distress, yet his declaration to them scarcely varies: "Your sins are forgiven." He says so very little because it's really so very much: God's will for us and God's work in us is gathered up in the pithy expression, "Your sins are forgiven." When the Apostles' Creed comes to speak of the Christian life, the whole of the Christian life, it uses only seven words: "I believe in the forgiveness of sins." For we are affirming the power and scope of God's grace to overturn estrangement on all the fronts and frontiers of life: our life with God, with our brothers and sisters, and with our profoundest selves.

Prayer

Gracious God, we praise you for your gospel. We rejoice in that "good news" which tells us the truth about ourselves only to soak us in a greater truth: we are the people upon whom you have poured out your own life. As your life infuses life into us, lift up our hearts and let our praise ascend to you.

We thank you today for the people you have given us for the well-being of our society, people whose work brings help and comfort to those caught in distressing circumstances. We lift them up to you at this time for your blessing:
>   *the social worker and the impoverished man;*
>   *the psychologist and the tormented woman;*
>   *the parole officer and the frightened convict;*
>   *the nurse and the homesick child;*
>   *the judge and the immature adolescent.*
>
> *Grant unto these people*
>   *the wisdom without which they cannot help or be helped,*
>   *the sensitivity without which hurt only increases,*
>   *the patience without which they shall quit in mid-*
>   *struggle.*

Yet we know, O God, that our deepest disorder only your gospel

*can set right. Therefore we intercede with you for all who hold up
Jesus Christ as the bread and water and wine of life. We plead
your blessing upon ministers,*

> *upon missionaries,*
> *upon theology students and professors,*
> *upon all who are entrusted with proclaiming our*
> > *Lord in whom we are forgiven,*
> > > *named,*
> > > *cherished, and*
> > > *given a dignity which no*
> > > > *one can take from us.*

*When they are discouraged, remind them that they need only be
faithful.
When they are frustrated, remind them that they must await
your time.
When they are super-confident, remind them that all Christian
growth is growth in humility.*

*We praise you that the faith in you which you have given us
suffuses us with your love for your people even as it quickens our
hope for the healing of the world. Increase our faith and love and
hope that we might praise you not only with our lips but also
with our lives, as we live for you who ever lives in us. Amen.*

DAY 34

REPENTANCE (1)
Mark 1:14-15

Breast-beating, tears, dredging up spiritual sludge—isn't this what "repentance" brings to mind? It's little wonder our society prefers to forget the word. After all, we aren't going to be helped by something which rubs our nose in our personal garbage pail as guilt and depression swell.

Nonetheless, the one who comes only to impart healing, help and wholeness summoned people to repent every day of his public ministry. The summons was—and is—urgent. "Don't put it off for a minute. Can't you see it's the only sensible thing for you to do?" The summons to repent is one of the major building blocks in our Lord's ministry. Pull it out, and his ministry would be unrecognizable.

Repentance, at bottom, isn't garbage pail-picking. Rather it's a change of mind with an attendant change in life. Both are needed. If there's only a change in our thinking, then we are racing our motor with the gears in neutral: lots of sound and fury (under the hood) but no advance. I remember sitting with an alcoholic fellow at 3:00 a.m. He knew he had a drinking problem. He understood the telltale signs, the progression of the ailment, the outcome. He knew what help was available. Sitting alongside us was another alcoholic who had been sober for several years. As our suffering friend insisted he had the situation turned around in his mind, the sober fellow kept asking him, "But what are you going to *do* about it?" Our friend did nothing. Racing the motor with the gears in neutral gets us nowhere. A change of mind without a change in life-direction falls short of repentance.

On the other hand, if there's a change in behaviour without a profound transformation of mind and heart then we have

---

merely conformed to peer pressure. As soon as a different
environment changes the peer pressure our behaviour will be
modified once more. This chameleon-likeness is obviously not
the repentance Jesus urges. He insists on both a change in
how we are thinking and a change in the course we are
pursuing.

Prayer

*Gracious God, we praise you today for your patience with us. You
come to us, speak to us, move within us, and then await our free
response to you. As we ponder our need of repentance, our
resistance to receive you and your readiness to embrace us, our
thanksgiving ascends to you for you have persisted in holding
open the door through which we must step and in calling out the
name—our own—which we must recognise.*

*Unstop our ears to the summons our Lord issued in the days of
his earthly ministry and continues to issue today, for we are
people whose mind must change:*

> *from unbelief to trust;*
> *from prayerlessness to adoration;*
> *from contempt to love;*
> *from vindictiveness to understanding;*
> *from bitterness to forgiveness;*
> *from rudeness to helpfulness;*
> *from snobbishness to humility.*

*We are people whose course must change as well. Then give us
grace to confirm the change we intend*

> *as we write the letter which bears our confession,*
> *as we make the phone call we have long feared,*
> *as we greet the person we have thought to be our enemy,*
> *as we renounce impediments to our Christian*
> > *development: laziness,*
> > > *self-indulgence,*
> > > *indifference to another's need,*
> > > *wilful deafness to the knock and*
> > > > *voice and look of our Lord.*

At the supper in the upper room when Jesus announced the coming betrayal, everyone cried, "Lord, is it I?"—except the one who did betray him. Then just as you save us from that breast-beating which does not honour you, save us also from that blindness which cannot see the betrayal which is ready-to-hand.

And just as our Lord taught us to ignore the speck in our neighbour's eye while the log juts out of our own, save us from the perverseness which maximizes the faults of others while minimizing our own.

Illuminate your kingdom so brightly for us, we ask, that repentance will appear the only sensible course for us to follow.

We end our prayer praising you for your humility which receives us at any time as we turn to you for any reason. We trust you to hold forever all who have looked to you and not been disappointed. Amen.

DAY 35

REPENTANCE (2)
Jeremiah 24:7; Isaiah 30:15

Repentance is a turning toward God. The Hebrew mind understands repentance to be a *returning* to God. When Israelites heard "repentance" they saw three clear pictures.

The first is that of an unfaithful wife returning to her husband. She has violated their marriage covenant, disgraced herself and humiliated her spouse. Yet his love for her, however wounded, remains undiminished and his patience unexhausted. As she turns to him she returns to longstanding love.

The second picture is that of idol-worshippers returning to the worship of the true God. In Hebrew, idols are literally "the nothings:" vacuous, empty, unsubstantial. Yet nothing is never *merely* *nothing*; nothing has terrific power, as both a lie and a vacuum attest. To turn to the worship of the living God is to return to truth, to reality, to solidity; in a word, to blessing so substantial that nothing can inhibit it.

The third picture is that of rebel subjects returning to their rightful ruler. Rebelling against rightful rule, they have plunged themselves into disorder and chaos, for it's proper authority that checks disorder and chaos in life. In turning to their rightful ruler they have returned to a trustworthy guide.

To repent, then, is to return to longstanding love, to truth, to legitimate authority.

Knowing all of this, however, we are yet prone to remain blind to the specific areas of our lives where (re)turning is in order. A good friend whom we trust, whose penetrating word we know not to be an attack upon us, can help us see. This person says to us gently, "Why do you keep putting your husband down when he needs affirmation?" "Why are you so harsh with your children at home but pretend such affection in public?" Because the mirror has been held up by someone we trust we shan't flee into defensiveness. Instead we shall soberly admit what the mirror reflects: we must turn to face the truth about ourselves and the claim of our Lord upon us, even as the face of longstanding love shines upon us ceaselessly.

Prayer

Eternal God, it is with joy and thanksgiving that we look to you at this time, for you have come to us as the Father who longs for his children, the Son who wants to render us all sons and daughters, the Spirit who hovers over all the creation. Hasten the day when the Son will be seen and acknowledged by all. Increase our love for you, our desire to obey you, and our gratitude to you, that we might be, and be seen to be, those who live for the praise of your glory.

We thank you for people who have reflected your character to us and who have kept before us a vision of the one to whom we must return again and again:
the faithful spouse who endured insult and disdain,
looking for the day when such love would beget
an answering love;
the parent who suffered the adolescent's rudeness, looking
for the day when maturity would engender
appreciation;
the child who held her peace when a playmate taunted
her cruelly, looking for the day when nastiness
would give way to friendship;
the teacher who insisted on diligence at school, looking for
the day when ignorance would give way to truth;
the soldier who spared the vanquished opponent, looking
for the day when enmity evaporated before mercy.

As we thank you for all who have helped us glimpse your character and purpose, give us grace to respond to you as we should, for you have permitted us the glimpse for just this end.

We intercede today for those who have not yet surrendered to truth, that you might move them as only you can:
> *the parent who abuses his dearest unknowingly;*
> *the schoolteacher unaware of the young person's sensitivity;*
> *the politician for whom graft is an instrument of office;*
> *the employee who cheats and the employer who exploits;*
> *the industrialist whose toxic waste is eclipsed by profit.*

Keep us looking to you whose heart is the heart of one who cares and whose voice calls us to our destiny and dignity.

It is because you are the God to whom we must turn and to whom we can return that we worship you, love you and serve you now. Amen.

DAY 36

REPENTANCE (3)
Romans 2:4

What moves us to repentance? Why would anyone gladly turn? One thing above everything else moves us to repent: the mercy and kindness of God. Paul writes, "Do you not know that God's kindness is meant to lead you to repentance?"

John the Baptist spoke much of repentance. His motive for it was fear, sheer fear. "The axe is laid to the root of the tree. The chaff is being burned in the fire. Repentance is the only route to survival." It's the big threat. Yet we falsify Jesus if we pretend that he never threatened. He did. Nonetheless, Jesus differs from John the Baptist in one important regard: for Jesus the decisive motive for repentance is the incomprehensible kindness of God. We joyfully repent as God's mercy floods us.

Our foreparents often erred in thinking that the big threat engineered repentance. The big threat doesn't change the human heart. To be sure it does coerce tolerable conduct, even as people hate the one who threatens them. How many adults are there who were emotionally bludgeoned into being models of middle-class convention and hated their parents for it? And how many adults, for the same reason, have grown up feeling the same way about God?

Our contemporaries (particularly our religious contemporaries), on the other hand, err in thinking that repentance is genuine only if we first disparage ourselves or purge ourselves or induce an unusual mental state. But to think we have to undergo a technique-ridden psycho-religious initiation is to cast aspersions on God's mercy and soak ourselves in anxiety: "I can't seem to get into the right 'space'." Nowhere does Jesus prescribe self-disparagement or psycho-religious self-preparation. He simply stands before us and assures us that his arms, the arms of the crucified, embrace everyone without exception, without condition and without hesitation.

Repentance, says Jesus, is coming to our senses, as the son in the far country came to his senses when he thought of the waiting father. It's to become a child again, for whom everything is received as gift. It's such an occasion of joy that it calls for a party, for celebration, for dancing.

Prayer

Loving God, we praise you for your kindness to us. We have seen your face in the face of Jesus your Son, who
>*ate with ne'er-do-wells,*
>*befriended the rejected,*
>*touched lepers,*
>*awakened the dead, and*
>*forgave sinners.*

As we think of how he moved among his people, let us ever find in your kindness that counsel and correction which never crush us.

We thank you that your mercy, wider than our need and deeper than our sin, is the mercy by which
>*you accept us without humiliating us;*
>*you forgive us without making us grovel;*
>*you claim us without burdening us;*
>*you love us without patronizing us;*
>*you seize us without stifling us;*
>*you send us out as prophets to plead with people for you,*
>>*and as priests to plead with you for people—*
>>>*without forsaking us.*

We praise you for the words of our Lord which have hung up in our minds pictures surrounding repentance that will never leave us:
>*the shepherd looking for the one lost sheep;*
>*the son coming to his senses and going home;*

the woman searching for the coin she has to have;
the man giving up everything for the pearl he cannot do
without.

*Just as your kingly nearness appeared in the ministry of our Lord
in his days upon earth, so may your kingdom loom so large before
us, so attractive, so necessary that we shall gladly leave our lesser
loves and loyalties to become citizens of a new city and dwellers
in a promised land.*

*Magnify our awareness of your unshakable kingdom, we ask, that
there might flow from us the praise of those whose God does all
things well. Amen.*

DAY 37

FAITH (1)
Genesis 32:22-28.

Everywhere Scripture links repentance and faith. But what is faith, anyway? Is it really "believing what you know isn't true," as the schoolboy said? Is it gullibility, the capacity for being "taken in?" Is it a matter of putting one's brain on the shelf, as those who recommend "blind faith" suggest? Faith is none of these.

Faith is encounter with God, engagement with God, communion with God, dialogue with God. It's not presumptuous chattiness, of course, not an off-putting overfamiliarity. But it's certainly involvement with God. God initiates this encounter as he graciously embraces us in Christ Jesus. In the power of his embrace we are awakened only to find that we can now embrace him *and want to.* Faith is holding fast to the one who has gripped us and whose grip on us will ever be stronger than our grip on him.

Our encounter with God can be riddled with turbulence. Our dialogue can take the form of anger as well as elation, accusation as well as adoration. Following his all-night wrestling with God, Jacob's name is changed to Israel: "he who contends with God." When we are rocked with crushing disappointment, unexpected grief, or sudden betrayal, it's natural and appropriate that we react as Abraham and Isaac, Moses and Jeremiah reacted: "Where were you when I needed you most? Why did you let it happen to me?" If we have never been angry with God then perhaps we have never been serious about him.

Our dialogue with God, unquestionably real, nevertheless can (and will) contain elements of confusion, moral deficiency and spiritual defectiveness. Nevertheless these elements don't

---

disqualify us as people of authentic faith. Our imperfection doesn't undermine the reality of our meeting. Remember, Peter lies. Martha fiddles with trivia even as the Master graces her home. James and John selfishly seek places of honour in the kingdom. John Wesley, a patron saint of the church catholic, lives for years amidst a marital turbulence that ends in separation and for which he shares more than a little blame. But none of it disqualifies people as disciples. Our encounter with God endures. For God seized us and spoke to us and won't give up on us. Our grip on God, however weak in itself, will ever be strengthened. The one who never wearies grasps us so as never to let us go.

Prayer

Gracious God, we praise you for your faithfulness to us. You keep the promises you make. You stand by us despite our doubt and disobedience. As often as we disbelieve in your persistence with us, turn our hearts and minds to see him who numbered himself among the transgressors for our sakes. For in him you declared yourself to be our advocate forever. As confidence in your faithfulness sinks deeper within us, let it bring forth the trust and love and praise we must give to you.

We thank you that you have always reached out to us, for you have always wanted us to be your covenant partner. Give us grace now to meet you in that encounter you want with us, to continue the conversation in which we find our true self, to know that communion which is hidden from the wise of this world but is cherished by the children of the light.

In the turbulence and triumphs of daily life, help us to learn from our ancestors in faith who have known our grief, our fragility, and our gladness, and who have wrestled with you through many long nights. They now shine like beacons, guiding us on our journey. We thank you

    for Sarah, who went forth to a strange land, with you as

her only security;
for Moses, who felt he could not lead your people but who
found your grace sufficient;
for an embarrassed woman, who touched our Lord and
found herself whole;
for Elijah, whom you would not allow to escape in the
cave forever.

We lift up before you, for your blessing, those dear to us whose
suffering has obscured their sense of your presence:
the man who has lost another job,
the mother whose children are hungry,
the couple whose son is chronically ill,
the daughter whose senile parent restricts her life and
quickens her guilt.
Shine so brightly upon these people, we ask, that they will see
their Lord whose dark night is an example for us all,
whose Easter victory must ever strengthen us,
whose constant care surrounds us even when we know
it not.

As we look to you who first sought us, we thank you for your
kindness and steadfastness, knowing that you will never fail or
forsake us. Amen.

DAY 38

FAITH (2)
2 Peter 1:5-8; 2 Timothy 4:13

Yet faith is more than an encounter or a dialogue. It's also knowledge. Imagine that you have just encountered Mozart's music. His music draws you in deeper and deeper as it captures you. As you are admitted to a world of new depths and new riches, you naturally want to learn something of Mozart, his relation to other composers, his place in the musical tradition. Conversely, as your knowledge increases you find that your profounder knowledge admits you to even greater depths and riches, and intensifies your delight still more.

So it is in our encounter with God. Once God has awakened us, drawn us, captivated us, we are impelled to gain understanding. As our understanding expands we find our delight in God increasing; in turn we are taken deeper into God's own life and acquainted with unforeseeable riches.

We must remember that knowledge is one dimension to Christian maturity. Where there is little advance in the knowledge of faith, people remain stunted. We can feel the frustration of the author of Hebrews who writes, "Milk is for babies; solid food is for grownups. So let's leave the elementary doctrines of Christ and go on to maturity, not laying the foundations all over again." In other words, can't we move beyond Grade One? Are we always going to be at the level of "Now I lay me down to sleep?" The stunted development of faith is no less grotesque or tragic than stunted development anywhere in life. And in fact people whose faith is undoubtedly genuine are going to have that faith strengthened, are going to possess greater certainty, are going to avoid being devastated or seduced by a religious huckster only as the knowledge dimension to faith is enlarged and deepened. Parents can provide Christian nurture for their children only as the parents themselves are learning more of the way and work and word of God.

Such knowledge is essential. Our Reformed foreparents spoke of the church as "the school of faith." Centuries before them a wise rabbi commented, "An hour of study is worth as much as an hour of prayer."

Prayer

Eternal God, the Psalmist has said that you are the one whose mercy endures forever. We praise you for that mercy which greeted us at our birth and will surround us at our death. Give us grace to cast ourselves on you, knowing that that which we entrust to you, you will keep safe until the day when faith gives way to sight and we know you as you now know us.

We thank you for those whom your Spirit touched and whom you inspired to write or paint, or play or sing, so as to honour you and lift us:

> *for Mozart and his* Requiem;
> *for Ella Fitzgerald and her gift of gospel song;*
> *for Christina Rossetti and her sensitive poetry;*
> *for C.S. Lewis and his haunting children's stories;*
> *for Stephen Schwartz and his "catchy"* Godspell.

As you have allowed all these to peer into the kingdom of your grace and truth, so let us share their vision in order that our hunger for you might be deepened and met, and our thirst for your rule sharpened and slaked.

We praise you for those little-known people who schooled us in faith when we were young and impressionable; unknown persons

> *who encouraged us to pray,*
> *who exemplified trust,*
> *who pointed out pitfalls,*
> *who focused our discernment,*

who combined the detachment of scholarship and the commitment of faith.

Their influence upon us is immeasurable, as our debt to them is unpayable. We thank you for them, and trust you to use us as you have used them, for after us come youngsters who have resolved to follow our Lord.

We plead with you for those whose growth in faith has been stunted by an image of deity that falsifies you,
>*by a friend who faltered when needed most,*
>*by gospel-presentations which insult intelligence,*
>*by a shrillness of spirit devoid of compassion.*

You alone, O God, are the searcher of hearts. You alone know when our lack of trust arises on account of our sin and when it is rooted in our being sinned against. Then to your mercy we commend such people now.

Just as you have brightened us with the knowledge of Christ you have granted to us, so continue to lead us in your will and way that we might be lights to those who live around us. And they will then give glory to you who are ever worthy of our praise. Amen.

DAY 39

FAITH (3)
Hebrews 10:39; 11:1-40; 12:1-2.

Yet faith is more than knowledge. It's a venture, a venture that has to be lived. Right here many people recoil. They have been so badly wounded, or fear being wounded, that venture is the last thing they want. They would much prefer to freeze whatever security they have now, gladly exchanging venture (with its unavoidable risk) for familiarity (with its unavoidable dullness.) The author of Hebrews recognizes the temptation with its attendant peril. He writes, "We are not of those who shrink back and are destroyed; we are of those who have faith...." The "we" who don't shrink back and shrivel up are those for whom faith is a life-venture under God.

My family spent a week at a summer cottage when I was seven years old. I longed to row the rowboat, but I was also afraid of the lake. I tied the boat to the dock with ten feet of rope. I rowed only two strokes when the boat jerked, drifted back to shore, and I began rowing again. I had done this several times when my father said, "If you want to row the boat and go somewhere, untie it." Immediately he saw my divided mind: I wanted to venture forth on the lake but was afraid. What could he do to quell my fear and free me to embark on the venture for which I longed? *He climbed into the boat with me.* I untied it and off we went *together.* If the Easter narrative of the two disciples on the road to Emmaus means anything it means that the same risen Lord who kept company with two men then keeps company with all his disciples now. And because he does, our anxiety is checked, at least enough to let us find life a venture with the one whom Scripture calls the "pioneer of our faith."

From time to time life will give us lemons. We'd like to throw them away, but we can't without throwing ourselves away with them. We can suck them, only to sour ourselves and others—or we can make lemonade. The one who is on the road with us is uniquely adept at making lemonade.

When we feel like the Israelites, plodding in the wilderness with the promised land still out of sight, the word given to Moses is the word we must hear: "Tell the people of Israel to go forward." For faith can't cease to be that venture which our Lord ever ventures with us.

Prayer

Gracious God, we praise you that you have never abandoned us and never will, for in Christ Jesus you have become that "friend who sticks closer than a brother." We bless you for your loyalty to us who are often disloyal to you. Change our fitful following into a discipleship which is always ready to obey our Lord, to sacrifice for his kingdom, to praise you for your bringing us from darkness to light and from death to life.

Because we too are caught in that suffering which none can escape, we approach with gentleness those whose suffering has reinforced unbelief; those who have witnessed

> *the lingering death of the very young child,*
> *the suffocation of the baby in the crib,*
> *the deepening depression of the disabled worker,*
> *the torment of the chronically insane.*

It is only you, O God, in the power of your Spirit who can crumble the barriers which affliction has raised. Then intensify the work of your Spirit, we ask, that those who find themselves flayed might know where there is healing for their wounded heart and strength for their weakened knees. We intercede for them now, trusting that you will render us effective instruments of your healing ministry.

We thank you for all who have cheered us along in the venture of faith: those whose wisdom redressed our unsound judgment;

> *those whose maturity tempered our impetuosity;*

those whose resilience dissolved our fearfulness;
those whose courage enabled us to venture forth;
those whose long experience of life and lemons and
lemonade convinced us that no situation is
opaque to you or hopeless to us.

We pray that we might be as much to all who look to us, that they might be moved to go forward with you.

You have guided, guarded and nourished us before. We trust you to do so again. And our praise ascending to you will be as constant as your goodness descending upon us. Amen.

DAY 40

LOVE (1)

Galatians 5:22-23; John 3:16; 1 John 4:8

It's through faith, of course, that we are born as Christians. Immediately however, we have to be clothed. After all, to remain unclothed is not only uncomfortable and even dangerous, it's humiliating. "Love is the clothing we are to put on," says Paul. Whenever and wherever we lack this clothing our nakedness is publicly exposed and we are rightly shamed.

But what is love? affection? friendship? being in love? In fact none of these is what the apostles mean by love. Affection, friendship, being in love are all natural loves; they grow naturally in human soil. But we are confronted with that love which is a fruit of the Spirit and faith, that love which God must root in us and nurture in us.

We learn of this love only as God's love seizes us. As God's love startles us we know that he has *done* something for us. He hasn't merely sent along best wishes or conveyed his positive feelings toward us. Instead he has loved us so as to give us— *himself.*"By this we know love,"writes John,"that he laid down his life for us."

And the "us" for whom he spent himself? "Sinners," explains the apostle tersely. 'We' were hostile to God, or at least indifferent to him, and certainly unappreciative and undeserving—yet he poured out himself for us.

Why did God do it? Why does he bother still? Simply because God is set upon our restoration. In response to God's magnanimity some people respond in love, a few with cursing, most with indifference. No one fully appreciates the depth and cost of God's love. Yet God is never discouraged. Nothing will induce God to stop loving us. Nothing can. The cross, where God, in not sparing his Son, didn't spare himself, is proof that God loves us more than he loves himself. God *is* love.

Our love can only be the mirrored reflection of his. Our love, the clothing which adorns the Christian, is a *deed*: we are to act on behalf of others, intending only their well-being, regardless of merit or appreciation.

Prayer

Eternal God, you always loved us with an everlasting love. Prophets who knew this anticipated the day when this love would become incarnate, embodied in the one you appoint. Apostles who knew this recalled the day when such love dwelt among them, full of grace and truth. Today we look to you who ever illumines our Lord for us, finding in his hold upon us a love that grips us, corrects us, cherishes us, and binds us to you for ever and ever.

We praise you that you have given yourself to us without reservation or qualification, for in Christ Jesus you poured yourself upon us
> *when we were enemies, that our hostility might vanish;*
> *when we were helpless, that we might find help in you;*
> *when we were estranged, that we might know the joy of*
> *coming home;*
> *when we were ungodly, that we might share the*
> *righteousness of Jesus our elder brother.*

We thank you for the people whose lives intersect ours and whose love is a conduit for your healing of our world:
> *the colleague who pardons our put-down even as we utter*
> *it;*
> *the mother with clamorous children who still has time for*
> *an aged parent;*
> *the harried father who lingers to console the little league's*
> *strikeout leader;*
> *the single parent whom neither hardship embitters nor*

loneliness sours.

We intercede today for those whose lives seem devoid of love. We know that our lifting them up to you for your blessing does not release us from their claim upon us. Then let our intercession be our reconsecration to you and our recommitment to those whom your love neither overlooks nor forgets. Let your holy fire burn ever hotter within us, consuming every impediment to our compassion.

Grant that the love which is poured into us might ever flow forth from us.

Bring before us, then, for our ministry:
> *the youngster with Attention Deficit Disorder whose scatteredness leaves him isolated;*
> *the ex-convict whose financial situation casts her upon so many others;*
> *the abused child whose inner wounds call out for solace;*
> *the alcoholic who cringes at being called weak or stupid when he is suffering terribly.*

It is because you love us without measure and without end that we can look to you and ever find the one who gathers us so very tenderly as you fit your approach to our need. Amen.

DAY 41

Love (2)

1 Corinthians 16:14; Ephesians 4:15; Colossians 2:2

Since love is something we do, let's look at some areas of life where love needs to permeate our doing.

Think of our speech. We are to "speak the truth in love." On the one hand, as small a book as the New Testament states five times that the Christian's "yes" is to be "yes" and his "no," "no". Our speech is to be transparent, not devious. There are to be no smoke screens, no deceitful footwork. On the other hand, this truth is always to be spoken in love. It's very easy to speak the truth and thereby stab someone. It's easy to speak the truth and wilfully, knowingly, destroy another person. In fact it's easy to do more damage by speaking the truth than by telling a lie. Who hasn't been bludgeoned by truth wielded as a weapon? Of course we can boast of our truth-telling as we crumble someone with it. We can speak the truth and yet subtly change our facial expression or alter our voice-inflection or add a little comment, all of which are as slight, apparently, as the stinger in a hornet, and all of which inject enough poison to cause pain. Our speech is supposed to edify. But speaking even the truth will edify only as we speak it in love. Our truth-telling must intend the well-being of another.

Let's look at Christian community. The congregation, Paul tells us, is "knit together in love." And love alone prevents it from unravelling. Love alone prevents it from flying apart. When you read the label on the tins of prepared meat (*Kam, Spork, Spam*, etc.), you learn that the meat product has been prepared from mechanically de-boned chicken or pork. Pig heads and chicken heads are placed in a centrifuge. The centrifuge then whirls around so fast that bits of meat fly off leaving the bones picked white. In any congregation there is much going on among many people in close proximity. There's always legitimate urgency to accelerate important business. In the course of the acceleration it's easy for people to be whirled around so fast (or feel they are) that the church community begins to fragment. A mechanically de-boned congregation is a rather sorry spectacle. The centrifugal force must be countered by a centripetal force: love. The counterforce is our determination to act for the well-being of others, regardless of merit or appreciation. All that we do must be done in love.

Prayer

Gracious God, it is of you that Jeremiah writes, "I have loved you with an everlasting love; therefore I have continued my faithfulness to you." Give us grace this day to know afresh your love for us, and knowing this to trust unreservedly your enduring faithfulness to us. Magnify our Lord Jesus Christ before us, we pray, that the faithfulness you demonstrated to him in raising him from the dead we shall see as the selfsame faithfulness you have pledged to us.

We confess that we have often been indifferent to your gift of love to us and your claim of love upon us. We admit we have allowed fear, hostility, and exasperation to drain our love as we met and received others in a spirit not of the Master. Hear us, then, as we search our hearts and lay before you the lovelessness that is pain to mention but poison to ignore:

> *the gesture whose contempt our disarming smile could not disguise;*
> *the glare whose hatred no one could mistake;*
> *the comment, apparently polite, whose sarcasm left someone shredded;*
> *the silence whose iciness stilled a criticism of us we should have heard.*

We make this our confession to you, knowing that your love will swallow up our lovelessness even as you grant us a new heart, a new mind, and a new spirit.

We pray that your love will infuse us, invigorate us, and inform us in those places where love is needed as parched earth needs water:

> *in our friendships, that we might not exploit them;*
> *in our families, that we might not treat them*
> *presumptuously or take them for granted;*
> *in our congregations, that we might value each person's contribution and pardon each person's shortcoming;*
> *in our workplace, that rancour might evaporate and concord flourish.*

The apostle insists, "Let all that you do be done in love." We look to you to soak us in that love which no one can exhaust; for only then will our deeds attest the deeds of him who went about doing good.

It is from you, great God of love, that we come.
It is for you, great God of love, that we live.
It is unto you, great God of love, that we shall return. Amen.

DAY 42

Love (3)

1 Corinthians 13.

Natural soil nurtures natural loves: affection, friendship, being in love. But anything natural, left to itself, begins to spoil and soon decays. Then plainly our natural loves need a preservative. The love that's a fruit of God's Spirit is the preservative.

Think of affection. It's certainly easier to make sacrifices for those of whom we are fond. Nevertheless, affection is fickle. It appears to be generous, even sacrificial, when really there are hidden strings attached. "I lived for my children. I gave them everything I could. Why do they have so little use for me now?" It could be that the children are simply ungrateful and cruel. More likely the affection lavished on the children was secretly (or not so secretly) manipulative. And now, at 30 or 40 years of age, they have put aside their feelings of guilt at thwarting dad, declaring in effect, that he's no longer a pliant victim of manipulation.

Affection spoils readily. A natural love, it will always decay unless a preservative is added. Love—acting on behalf of another, intending only that person's well-being, regardless of merit or appreciation—this alone preserves affection as *affection.*

Think of being in love. Anyone who has been in love knows there's nothing like it. Only the sourest person dashes cold water on being in love. The "fit" which two people find in each other is nothing to belittle. But being in love spoils readily too. Two people are usually content to stare at each other—for as long as their mutual intoxication allows them to overlook defects in each other. One day, however, as they stare at each other they feel less like lovebirds and more like X-ray

---

machines. Now the irritating character defects stand out sharply. Soon this is all they can see.

A preservative is needed. Many are suggested, such as a weekend in a hotel. A weekend locked up with a character defect? Surely a better preservative is that love which is the fruit of God's Spirit. Being in love is saved from decay as two people *do* something for each other, intending only the other's well-being.

It's no wonder Paul writes, "Make love your aim." For this love is the clothing which spares the Christian sickly chills and shame. This love mirrors the love of him who first loved us, without regard to our merit or appreciation.

Prayer

Gracious God, it is Hosea who hears you say,
>   *"How can I give you up, O Ephraim?*
>   *How can I hand you over, O Israel?*
>   *My heart recoils within me;*
>   *my compassion grows warm and tender."*

We rejoice, O God, that not even our waywardness can induce you to give up on us, your people. We do not come to you today to trade on the constancy of your compassion, yet we do approach you, grateful that you are the same yesterday, today and forever.

Move upon us afresh, in this time of prayer, that
>   *our fractious spirit you will subdue,*
>   *our darkened understanding you will illumine, and*
>   *our stony heart you will render a heart of flesh.*
As we reflect upon the love of our Lord, so magnify his love in us that we shall be agents of that love which
>   *resists a family's proneness to fragment;*
>   *resists a community's narrow self-concern;*
>   *resists a society's slide toward violence; and*
>   *resists a nation's vainglorious boasting.*

*We plead with you to expand in us that love which alone makes
us agents of reconciliation, for only such love can reconcile*
> *ethnic person and WASP,*
> *anglophone and francophone,*
> *welfare recipient and high-bracket taxpayer,*
> *environmentalists whom nature needs and*
> > *industrialists whom employment needs.*

*Because it is our conviction, as it is the apostle's, that love never
ends, we ask you to enlarge within us*
> *the love which bears all things, and therefore does not*
> > *resent the burdens which cannot be dropped;*
> *the love which believes all things, and therefore sees every*
> > *man and woman embraced in Christ;*
> *the love which hopes all things, and therefore will not*
> > *wilt in the face of discouragement;*
> *the love which endures all things, and therefore is neither*
> > *exhausted nor withdrawn.*

*Knowing that you keep the promises you make, O God, we trust
you to grant to us what you have ordained for us. At the
beginning of each day as at its ending, we shall know your power
at work within us, for you are able to do far more abundantly
than all that we ask or think. Amen.*

DAY 43

JOY (1)
1 Peter 1:3-9; John 16:22

"Fun in the sun," says the poster; "Play now, pay later." There is certainly nothing wrong with pleasure. God has provided ever so much that gives us pleasure.

Nevertheless, pleasure isn't the same as joy. Pleasure depends on circumstances and therefore largely on chance. Pleasure is fleeting: toothache, headache or travel sickness can evaporate it. What's more, pleasure is subject to the law of diminishing returns. What gave us pleasure yesterday gives us less today and less again tomorrow. More and more stimulation is required to maintain our pleasure levels. Pleasure is precarious.

Joy is something else. Paul says more about joy in his Philippian letter than in any other, and this letter he wrote while in prison. Joy doesn't depend on circumstances. Neither is it subject to the law of diminishing returns. While pleasure is linked to our fondness for things, joy arises from our delight in God. "Without having seen him you love him," writes Peter of his Lord; "You believe in him and you rejoice with unutterable and exalted joy."

Joy is contentment. Joy is the satisfaction of longing (not of desire), of that longing so deep in the human heart that there can be none deeper. We must never think that by feeding desire we can satisfy longing. Ultimately we long for God.

When we were children and became lost, all we wanted was to get home. Adults who noticed our upset were kind to us, and even gave us candy. But no lost child, however sweet her tooth, would ever confuse the pleasure of candy with the joy of going home. When Jesus wishes to infuse us with joy he tells three pity parables: a shepherd looks for a lost sheep and rejoices that he has found it; a homemaker with no grocery money to spare turns the house inside out and rejoices that she has found her coin; a father rejoices to see his son coming up the road. Shepherd, homemaker and father—all describe the God who rejoices at the restoration of his dear people. Our joy at going home is a reflection of God's joy at having us home. To his disciples Jesus says, "Your hearts will rejoice. And no one will take your joy from you." No one can.

Prayer

Eternal God, the prophet Isaiah insists that
> *in returning and rest we shall be saved,*
> *in quietness and in trust shall be our strength.*
We approach you at this time
> *certain that you will receive us,*
> *confident that you will hear us,*
> *convinced that you will save us.*

Subdue within us our anxieties,
> *our distractions,*
> *our preoccupations, and*
> *all that impedes our worship of you.*

Give us grace to cast ourselves upon your mercy and your truth,
for then you will cause us
> *to stand forth boldly in your world,*
> *to walk courageously the road you have appointed for us,*
> *to shine clearly as lights that reflect him who is the light*
> > *of life.*

We thank you today for the good gifts of your creation which you
have given us to enjoy:
> *the mountain range whose grandeur makes our hearts*
> > *ache;*
> *the ocean surge which leaves us wordless;*

the stranger's smile which melts our coldness;
the child's frankness which refreshes our spirit;
the friend's affection which lightens our burden.

Our gratitude swells yet again as we ponder the joy you have lent us:
the joy of pardon amidst sin's perversity;
the joy of peace in the thick of turbulence;
the joy of comfort in the midst of grief;
the joy of victory in the face of temptation;
the joy of life eternal in the midst of our dying.

We intercede today for those whom this day finds sad and discouraged:
the woman whose dismissal spells hardship for her children;
the teenager whose physique elicits the cruellest taunts;
the parents whose long-awaited baby has been born deformed;
the politician whose compromise has left him hating himself.
It is your word of truth, O God, which assures these people of your availability.
It is your word of mercy which forgives and heals.
It is your word of hope which moves them another step along the road of life.
Then speak your own word to them, we ask, and magnify that word in their hearing until they know once again that they are people with whom you are pleased.

We conclude our prayers in the name and Spirit of him who assures us that no one seeks or asks or knocks in vain. For you who have commanded your people to pray will never turn us away empty-handed. Amen.

DAY 44

JOY (2)

Romans 14:17.

Yet joy is much more than feeling good. Joy has the profoundest consequences for our daily existence. Joy, for instance sheds temptation. Temptation is really a form of "fallout" given off in the conflict between the evil one and the holy one of God. It drifts everywhere. It can't be avoided. Does it stick? Does it irradiate us? People who are chronically discontent shed temptation much less readily. After all, to be discontent is to be suggestible, prone to suspend sound judgement and ignore wise counsel. Temptation sticks and penetrates precisely when pleasure is waning and joy hasn't yet taken hold. Joy, the profoundest contentment in life, disperses temptation.

Think about anger. There are situations where anger is appropriate, even necessary. Jesus was angry on many occasions. Yet the apostle's caution is in order: "Be angry, but do not sin." Temptation has taken root in us when our anger outstrips the offence or when our anger degenerates into resentment, into a vendetta aimed at crumbling someone else. Joy sheds the floating temptation which has alighted on us. Joy, in fact, can prevent any temptation from irradiating us.

Everyone knows that the grass turns brown in the midsummer heat wave. The grass isn't dead. Undeniably, however, it's dry and brown. Still, it was green before and it will be green again. To tear up the lawn just because it's brown at this moment would be utterly foolish. From time to time all human relationships become rather dry and turn somewhat brown. They were green before and they will be green again. One thing we don't do is tear up the relationship and discard it. There's always the temptation to do this, however, and to do it with one human relationship in particular: marriage. It has dry/brown periods as well. Joy, our profoundest contentment, ensures that the temptation to do something foolish doesn't take root in us.

To know the God whose joy no one takes from us is to be armed adequately against temptation.

Prayer

Gracious God, it is good to get up and see the sun risen in the sky. Yet how much better it is to get up and know the Son of Man risen from the dead. Hold up before us, we ask, the one whom you have given to us as Saviour and Lord, that we might know ourselves included in his risen life, and by it set upon that Way which we know to be Truth. Increase our faith until that day when faith gives way to sight. For we, together with all your people, await this day when we shall hunger no more, neither thirst any more. And on this day, with one voice, we shall cry, "Worthy art thou, our Lord and God, to receive glory and honour and power."

Today we remember before you, for their strengthening, those whom temptation assails from within and assaults from without:
>   *the bank employee whose fingers itch as his personal debt
>   mounts;*
>   *the teacher whose spirit sours as parents fault her for a
>   child's failure;*
>   *the company president whose bookkeeping "fudge" silences
>   creditors;*
>   *the factory worker who is courted by dishonest
>   management and a dishonest union;*
>   *the minister whose carelessness is close to moral collapse.*

For all such people we plead your grace, trusting you to convince, convict, and support them as you alone can.

We praise you for our Lord Jesus Christ, and especially for the

example he left us. For his trust in you remained steadfast
    when he was tried in the wilderness;
    when his family was ashamed of him;
    when his disciples misunderstood him;
    when rulers conspired against him;
    when mockers ridiculed him;
    when soldiers abused him; and
    when you, his Father, were cut off from him.
As we learn of him, grant that we shall not withdraw our trust in
you, even as we shall not curse our circumstances. Let us find in
your faithfulness to us all that we need to remain faithful to you.

And as we all long for you, draw us to you,
                enfold us in you,
                open our eyes to you.
For then we shall cry with the hymnwriter,
    "Thou, O Lord, art all I want;
    More than all in thee I find." Amen.

DAY 45

Joy (3)

1 Thessalonians 1:2-7; Colossians 1:11.

Joy makes Christian character rich, credible and attractive. Joy makes faith winsome and contagious. Paul prays that the Christians in Colosse will be strengthened for all endurance and patience "with joy." Endurance and patience are certainly necessary, but they are never enough. Where joy is lacking, endurance becomes resignation: "I can only grit my teeth and hang on." The word "endurance" suggests sporting contests like marathon running or 30-day bicycle racing. The picture flashing before our minds is that of the athlete who is near exhaustion, near emotional collapse; in a word, grim.

There is much in life that we simply have to endure. What's more, very few human problems are solved; most have to be borne. Will our endurance be grim? Or will there be a richness, a credibility, an attractiveness about our Lord's work within us? Joy lends winsomeness to Christian character.

Affliction besets everyone. Sometimes it's only a drip, drip, drip; more of a nuisance than anything else. At times it's a flood. What does affliction do to someone's character? Does it render this person grim or sour or nasty? Or is affliction the occasion when the person's character shines with a richness and an attractiveness which we should otherwise never see? Does genuine joy lend a credibility to Jesus Christ which renders argument about him superfluous and eloquence unnecessary? Catherine Booth, co-founder of The Salvation Army, was the genius behind the organization. From age fourteen until her death at age sixty-one she never knew a day without pain, often considerable pain. Catherine Booth had an uncanny effectiveness when she spoke to large gatherings of East London men and women whose degradation beggared description. She didn't have a plastic smile that could be pasted on for the newspaper photographer. Yet she was possessed of a joy in the midst of her pain that quickened faith and hope in people who had long since given up on themselves. In her joy they saw the beginning of theirs. In her joy they knew that the way out—their homecoming—was real and ready-to-hand.

Joy will ever lend richness to Christian character and credibility to our Lord himself as he continues to form himself in us who are his people.

Prayer

Eternal God,

> *you are Creator; we owe our very breath to you;*
> *you are Judge; we cannot hide our innermost self from*
> *you;*
> *you are Redeemer; we are blessed in the sacrifice of your*
> *Son;*
> *you are Lord; we acknowledge your claim upon us;*
> *you are Spirit; we are nourished and freshened as gently*
> *as the softest rain.*

In the time we have set aside to meet with you now, let us see you again in your unsearchable riches, for we shall know again that your grace and truth are as diverse as our needs.

We come to you as a hungry person comes for food;
> *as a weary person comes for rest;*
> *as a beleaguered person comes for peace;*
> *as a cheerful person comes to one with whom she*
> *can share her elation.*

Peter has told us that you are "many-splendoured." As we reflect upon the diverse dimensions of our life and the variegated richness of your grace, we are impelled to endorse his acclaim. And just as Paul was certain that you could supply all our needs

*in Christ Jesus, so let us add our testimony to theirs, that the
strugglers and doubters around us may hear our common witness
to our common Lord, and may cherish the experience common to
God's people.*

*We thank you for those who have known affliction, whose pain
threatened to eclipse their trust in you, yet whose joy your Spirit
magnified until they were constrained to say, "Great is the Lord,
and greatly to be praised." So it is we bless you*
> *for Catherine booth, whose love for city slum-dwellers
> was uncontrived;*
> *for Dietrich Bonhoeffer, whose cheerfulness brightened
> many in a concentration camp;*
> *for Corrie Ten Boom, who can tell us of the cost of
> forgiveness;*
> *for Mary, mother of our Lord, whose wounded heart has
> inspired the devotion of thousands.*

*For all these people and for all who are like them, we thank you
at this time, praising you that their contentment in you kept them
faithful to you even unto death.*

*Because we are commanded to praise you, O God, and because we
are constrained to praise you, we conclude our prayers in the
Spirit of Zechariah, whose mouth was opened,*
> *whose tongue was loosed and
> whose heart leapt before you, his God and
> Saviour. Amen.*

DAY 46

Patience (1)
James 5:7

"Lord, give me patience—and give it to me *now*." We chuckle at the sign on someone's desk. We step into an elevator and immediately push the button like a woodpecker drilling a tree trunk when once would have been sufficient. While the only damage done here is damage to our blood pressure, that is surely damage enough.

Yet there's an impatience even more dangerous. The captain of the *Titanic* was racing his ship through iceberg-bound water, in a fog, because he wanted to set a record for a transatlantic crossing. The "unsinkable ship" foundered. Leaders pushed a group of schoolboys to continue canoeing in unsafe conditions in order to save time. Fourteen drowned. "Speed is the white person's curse," a First Nation spokesperson commented laconically. So important is patience (and so rare is it) that Paul lists it as a fruit of God's Spirit. God himself must work it in us.

God can work patience in us only because he is patient himself. God manifests patience only because he *is* patience. "The Lord is merciful and gracious, slow to anger and abounding in *steadfast* love." (Psalm 103:5)

We know that the people of Israel were called and gathered that they might be the cradle in which the Saviour of the world was laid, and out of which he came with blessing for all. We nod in assent, forgetting that 1500 years elapse from Israel's earliest calling to the birth of Jesus. We read the 53rd chapter of Isaiah, "He was despised and rejected by men; a man of sorrows and acquainted with grief...and the Lord has laid on him the iniquity of us all." We insist that Jesus Christ is the fulfillment of the prophet's word. We lose sight of the

---

fact that hundreds of years elapse between the utterance and its fulfillment. To learn this much is to understand that God is patient beyond our imagining.

Some early Christians who were suffering terribly railed against Peter, "Why doesn't God do something about our plight? Why doesn't God end history and bring in the age-to-come? Why is he so slow about his promise?" "God isn't *slow*," Peter replies; "God is *patient*." There's a difference. With our maker a thousand years are but a day.

The fruit of patience can appear in us because the root of patience is the God who is patient.

Prayer

O gracious Lord, the Psalmist has written, "From everlasting to everlasting thou art God." We praise you that your mercy greeted us at our birth and will surround us at our death. We praise you that you do not weary and your love does not wane, for you are the God whose patience waits for us, weeps over us and woos us. Hear us as we come to you to receive from you all that you long to give us, to tell us, and to do through us.

In the light of your long-suffering we confess the sin of our impatience and deplore its consequences:
> *our cutting word when someone moved more slowly than we liked;*
> *our demeaning manipulation when someone took more pains than we thought necessary;*
> *our heavy-handed coercion when our agenda fell behind schedule;*
> *our slipshod work, as useless as it was quick.*

We confess that our impatience finds us doing what hurts other people and undermines their trust, even as it delays the appearance of your kingdom's righteousness and peace.

Admit us to your vision for your world and to your patience with it so that we might be servants whose obedience is contented and cheerful.

Alert as we are to our impatience and its wreckage, save us as well from substituting impatience with
> *the laziness which disdains exertion,*
> *the selfishness which resists sacrifice,*
> *the dullness which is blind to opportunities,*
> *the fear which cowers before risk,*
> *the callousness which remains unmoved by pain.*

Even as you share your patience with us, sensitize us to the crises which demand trenchant perception, resolute decision and courageous action.

Grant us to see, we plead,
> *your kingdom instead of our schemes,*
> *your love instead of our self-concern,*
> *your mercy instead of our scorn.*

Imbue us with that Spirit who can
> *wait until the son returns,*
> *wait until the coin is found,*
> *wait until the sheep is restored to the fold.*

We rest ourselves in you for whom a thousand years are but a day, for you are the Eternal One whom we cannot escape,
> *whom we do not wish to avoid,*
> *and whose patience will ever be our*
> *peace. Amen.*

DAY 47

PATIENCE (2)
Ephesians 4:1-3.

Certainly we need patience with people. It seems that we are always colliding with others. Even when we are attempting to help them, even as we are making no little sacrifice for them, our frustration drives us to give up on them. It seems that some of them are trying to be awkward.

There was a player on my hockey team who looked magnificent in practice. When the rubber pylons were placed on the ice five yards apart he would stickhandle through them at full speed, dipsy-doodling like Wayne Gretzky, then roar in on the net and unleash a shot that would kill a horse. But in game situations he couldn't do anything. It turns out a rubber pylon isn't an opponent bent on mayhem.

All of us are interacting all the time with new people, new events and new ideas. In other words, we change. We occupy different space. None of us is exactly what we were ten years ago. We're all moving all the time. Any number of people can find their way around a rubber pylon that never moves. But what are we supposed to do about people who are shifting positions all the time, as we are ourselves? What's more, even the person whom we like most will hit out at us from time to time. We shall be wounded. What next? Only patience can keep us in the relationship we have entered upon; only patience can hold us to the commitment we have made to others.

We mustn't think that patience means we fold our hands, do nothing, and watch the world go by with the indifference of a cow chewing her cud. Cud-chewing indifference isn't patience and it isn't a fruit of the Spirit. Paul reminds Timothy of what the younger man is to do: convince, rebuke, exhort. Then he adds, "Be unfailing in patience." When patience fails, an attempt at convincing becomes verbal assault; rebuke (correction) becomes carping; exhortation becomes pestering. Of course there's an urgency about any work that is worth our time and talent. But without patience urgency becomes frenzy.

Paul lists fifteen characteristics of love (1 Corinthians 13.) The first is patience. Without patience, love self-destructs before the remaining fourteen can appear.

Prayer

Gracious God, we approach you today because you first approached us. Come to us again, we ask, and penetrate us afresh with your Spirit that our Lord we shall see,
> *his summons we shall heed, and*
> *his command we shall obey.*
This we ask in the confidence that you want to stamp upon us the one who is the very stamp of your nature and the reflection of your glory.

We intercede today for those who bear grave responsibility and whose patience or impatience will spell blessing or bane:
> *government leaders, who have in their hands more power*
>> *than we can imagine;*
> *labour negotiators, who influence profoundly our social*
>> *relations;*
> *ambassadors and diplomats, who implicate all of us in*
>> *their deliberations;*
> *military commanders, whose decisions are weighty*
>> *beyond our telling.*

You have commanded us to pray for those in authority over us. We do so now, trusting you to supply them with the wisdom, courage and compassion to fulfill the mandate you have given them.

We praise you for those whose patience has been a window

---

through which we glimpsed your purpose and presence:
> *the counsellor who heard us when we were tearful and*
> > *frantic;*
> *the friend whom our tongue flayed but who did not*
> > *respond in kind;*
> *the child who saw our dishonesty yet kept on loving us;*
> *the colleague who endured our mistakes while we learned*
> > *the new job;*
> *the spiritual advisor who led us deeper year by year*
> > *into you our God.*

In your kindness you have given us these people that you might support us, strengthen us, and conform us to him whose life must one day be ours. Rejoicing in your good gifts, we thank you for them, even as we ask to be instruments of your work in those whose lives intersect ours.

As with you the day began, so with you may this day end. For you are the one whose mercy endures for ever. Amen.

DAY 48

PATIENCE (3)
1 Timothy 1:12-16.

Certainly we need to be patient with ourselves. If we are at all serious about our Christian growth it's easy to become discouraged with ourselves. In fact it's easy to become dismayed when we look in on ourselves and see not only the fruits of the Spirit but also jungle savagery. We assume we are progressing toward Christian maturity until one day we see that more of the jungle remains within us than we guessed just because something lurking in that jungle has flashed out. Startled, we feel our discipleship is shoddy (still shoddy, after all these years.) Paralyzing disappointment now laps at us.

Not so long ago we Shepherds had my wheelchair-bound mother-in-law with us. The children had been wrangling. They had also been eating a great deal of candy. I had spent half an hour preparing lunch, and as all sat down at the table, first one child turned up her nose at the food and then the other. Next they asked if they could have a cookie. Then they began fighting over a package of lifesavers. I "boiled over" and began hollering at them like someone deranged. At the height of my rage I picked up the package of lifesavers and threw it—anywhere—just threw it as hard as I could. It hit my mother-in-law square in the forehead. The violent action and the violent speech froze terror and shock on her face. I knew at once what her frightened, uncomprehending look meant: there flashed before her the male violence from which she had suffered and had endeavoured to escape. My rage brought all of this back for her; hence the terror. And her *minister* son-in-law had done it; hence the shock. Something had flashed out of the jungle recesses.

We assume we are advancing in the Christian life as readily

and as easily as water flows downhill, until one day a situation develops that indicates the jungle within us to be so dense as to hide from sight whatever Spirit-fruit is germinating as well. It's no wonder we are prone to lose patience with ourselves. Then we must look away from ourselves to our Lord and note how patient he is with his disciples. He bears with their inconsistency, their petty-mindedness, their undisguisable self-contradiction, their inflated pretensions to spiritual gianthood when every day they expose themselves as pipsqueaks. Paul knows that with him Christ has had to display perfect patience. Our Lord will ever do as much with us. Then we must begin to display the selfsame patience with ourselves.

Prayer

Loving God, the hymnwriter cries,
*   "O to grace, how great a debtor,*
*   daily I'm constrained to be."*

We come to you today aware that your grace has called us into the company of your dear Son. In his company your grace has given us new standing with you, new nature within ourselves, and a new name before the world. Grant that your grace poured ceaselessly upon us might elicit unending gratitude from us. And grant that our gratitude will be not only the praise of our lips but also the offering of our lives. Help us now to give ourselves to you who have given yourself to us.

Since you have called us into your church in calling us to Jesus, we plead with you for our own denomination that you might correct it, heal it, strengthen it and use it as the pattern of what you long to do for the whole world. We intercede especially
*   for its leaders, that those who are our shepherds will*
*   hear the Shepherd's voice above the clamour*
*   of stress and strife;*
*   for the officials of its several divisions, that they who*

are entrusted with so much will do the
truth of the gospel;
for those whose special responsibility is the anxiety
and anguish of congregations and ministers;
for the little-known people of the offices: typists and
clerks, bookkeepers and caretakers, who are
rarely noticed yet always essential;
for members who are confused by the collision
between the gospel and the principalities.

We pray that schism will not divide us, nor bitterness engulf us, nor hostility overwhelm us. We ask that we who are one in Christ may be one before the world as well.

We praise you for your covenant faithfulness which has held and healed your church through long days
of heresy, when the truth of God was distorted,
of superstition, when self-serving magic seemed
attractive,
of prejudice, when people were mistreated because of
gender or colour or nationality,
of blindness, when peripheral matters were
preoccupations.

Knowing that you will never forsake your church, we trust you to supply what is lacking in our life, our witness and our love. Sharpen our hearing of that word which we must ever heed.

Gracious God, you have promised that the powers of death will not prevail against your church. Assured that you will honour your promise, we bow before you again and glorify you anew. Amen

DAY 49

THE CONSUMMATION

1 Thessalonians 4:13-18; 1 Corinthians 11:26;
Philippians 1:6; 1 John 3:2

The Word became flesh. The Incarnation *happened*: once, once for all. The Incarnation isn't repeated. There's no need for it to be repeated. All that our Lord came to do he accomplished. "It is finished."

Nevertheless, he who came once (for all) comes to us again and again in the power of his Spirit. He in whom God invaded human history isn't confined to a past occurrence. He comes to comfort and challenge us, his people, as often as we look to him or he overtakes us.

At the same time Scripture unambiguously insists that our Lord "will come again." When the apostles say this they don't mean that Jesus Christ is now absent and must somehow become present. Instead we are to understand that our Lord, who is known only to people of faith at this time, will be manifest to everyone. As he himself is manifested to the world his truth, his rule, his power, his love will be manifested as well.

The photographer in her darkroom puts a negative in her enlarger and shines a picture onto a piece of photographic paper. The image is now imprinted onto the paper. Someone coming into the darkroom, however, who looked at the paper would see nothing at all, and would conclude that it was no different from any sheet of blank paper. Then the paper is dipped into a tray of chemicals. In a few seconds a picture emerges. It stands forth, every detail sharply defined and recognizable. Really, it was there all the time. To say that our

Lord will come again is to say that he, together with his rule, his truth, his love (now known only to his people) will become manifest to the entire world. It's not that something spooky will occur. Rather, what was there all the time in him will be seen to be here.

What then? All that our Lord has done for his world and in the hearts of his people will be brought to its consummation. He will complete that good work which he has begun in us. Our universe, which has groaned (like a woman in the last stages of labour) in expectation of the birth of a new heaven and a new earth, will groan no longer. The tormented of the world, whose torment has obscured their apprehension of the world's rightful ruler, will find relief. The church's shame at its unfaithfulness will be dispelled.

Indeed, we shall "…hunger no more, neither thirst any more; the sun shall not strike us, nor any scorching heat. For the lamb in the midst of the throne will be our shepherd, and he will guide us to springs of living water; and God will wipe away every tear from our eyes" (Revelation 7:16-17). In a word, we shall be like him, for we shall see him as he is (1 John 3:2).

Prayer

Eternal God, you called the universe into existence and you entered human history in Jesus of Nazareth; you will bring that history to completion as you sum up all things in him.

Rivet our attention upon our Lord who was and is and is to come, that his coming might find us doing the work of the kingdom, servants who have expected their master's return.

We praise you that the river of life ends in the ocean and not in a swamp,
that the pilgrim who is beckoned by the light in the distance doesn't lie forgotten in the dark,

that the citizen who is pressing on to the heavenly
kingdom does not find his end in a grave
of earth.
In all the trials and tempests of life, illumine for us the one who
is our life, for he is the road we travel, our companion on the
journey, and the destiny we await.

We thank you that there is a future, and it is Christ's.
Give us grace to move toward him who will make all things
new.
We thank you that there is a rule, and it is Christ's.
Give us grace to obey upon earth him whose authority none
shall deny in heaven.
We thank you that there is a fellowship, and it is Christ's.
Give us grace to embrace with joy the whole people of God
whose destination we share.

As we await the coming of our Lord who is with us even now,
let us see his kingdom, hidden from the world but visible
to faith;
let us do the work which others disregard but which we
find fruitful;
let us commend the Saviour whom some disdain but who
is life to us;
let us live like those who watch and wait for the one we
long to meet.

O faithful God, in raising Jesus Christ from the dead you
guaranteed his final manifestation, even as you guaranteed rest
for all who labour and are heavy laden. Until the glorious day of
his appearing, sustain all whose difficulty his coming shall
relieve:
the insane who have lost everything but their reason;
the tormented whose pain no drug can still;
the hungry whose days are spent in misery;
the refugees who shall have a home at last.
All such we entrust to you, knowing that you will grant unto

them what they never found on earth.

Eternal God, you have quickened our zeal for the day when we shall stand before you without spot or blemish. Then increase our faith, deepen our repentance, magnify our ardour, that our prayer may be the cry of our ancestors, "Come, Lord Jesus." And unto you we ascribe all glory, honour, dominion and power, now and ever. Amen.

Printed in the USA
CPSIA information can be obtained
at www.ICGtesting.com
CBHW032054250724
12187CB00021B/108